OXFORD ENGLISH FOR CAREERS

COMMER

Martin Hobbs and Julia Starr Keddle

Teacher's Resource Book

OXFORD
UNIVERSITY PRESS

OXFORD
UNIVERSITY PRESS

Great Clarendon Street, Oxford OX2 6DP

Oxford University Press is a department of the University of Oxford.
It furthers the University's objective of excellence in research, scholarship,
and education by publishing worldwide in

Oxford New York

Auckland Cape Town Dar es Salaam Hong Kong Karachi
Kuala Lumpur Madrid Melbourne Mexico City Nairobi
New Delhi Shanghai Taipei Toronto

With offices in

Argentina Austria Brazil Chile Czech Republic France Greece
Guatemala Hungary Italy Japan Poland Portugal Singapore
South Korea Switzerland Thailand Turkey Ukraine Vietnam

OXFORD and OXFORD ENGLISH are registered trade marks of
Oxford University Press in the UK and in certain other countries

First published 2006
2010 2009 2008
10 9 8 7 6 5 4 3 2

ISBN: 978 0 19 456976 7

Printed in Spain

ACKNOWLEDGEMENTS

Art & photo editing by Pictureresearch.co.uk

*The author and publisher are grateful to the following for their permission to reproduce
photographs*: Alamy p.77 (David Young-Wolff); Getty Images p.85 (man seated /
Taxi Japan / Ryuichi Sato), (woman in jeans / Photonica / Jason Todd); Royalty
Free cover (Punchstock / Stockbyte), pp.75 (MedioImages), 85 (woman in
suit / MedioImages), man standing / Purestock), 89 (Stockbyte Platinum), 97
(Blend Images); Science Photo Library p.93 (Philipe Psaila)

Contents

Introduction

Commerce is designed for students who intend to get a job in a business context. It prepares them for a wide range of business situations, develops telephone and communication skills, and provides them with background in major business concepts.

Start up

This is designed as a warm-up activity to the unit. It often introduces key vocabulary or concepts, and should be used to get students to focus on the topic.

9 to 5

This section occurs in alternate units. It presents and practises functional and situational language in simple business contexts. It is set in an advertising agency. There are three main characters: Richard (the manager), Lisa Scacchi (his new Personal Assistant), and Joe (her colleague). The activities move from the presentation of target language to activities and role-plays that practise the language in meaningful contexts.

Call centre

This section presents the basic language of making and receiving telephone calls. There is a listening task after which students are asked to analyse the interaction and then do a speaking task using the target language. It is linked to Pronunciation exercises where necessary.

It's my job / Company profile

These occur in alternate units, and provide visual input and text. They are all based on authentic interviews and sources and are designed to be of interest to the students as they stand with only minimal tasks. In 'It's my job', students will read about a variety of young people in different business environments and gain insight into the skills required.

General focus questions for 'It's my job' and 'Company profile' are: *What do you think his / her job involves? What skills and experience does he / she need? Would you like to do it? What do you know about this company? Would you like to work there?*

As an ongoing project, encourage the class to build up a portfolio of other 'It's my job' or 'Company profile' features.

Business know-how

Increasingly in business, it is not enough to have experience or qualifications. Employers are also looking for staff with strongly developed soft skills. These skills include teamwork skills, self motivation, flexibility, leadership skills, organizational skills, and interpersonal skills. This section is designed to introduce these skills gently to the students through entertaining activities.

Project

This encourages students to take an active role in the learning process, working in pairs or groups to explore topics and find out more about companies.

Projects can be set as homework assignments, but it is worth spending time in class preparing students for the task. Students are usually required to use search engines such as www.google.com or www.altavista.com to find information. Help can also be given by brainstorming some standard places where they can gather information.

Top margin

This top part of the page contains facts, statistics, and quotes. These are optional extras and can be used to add variety and interest to your lessons, or provide additional material for strong students who are 'fast finishers'. Sometimes they have an associated question, and ways of exploitation include asking whether your students are surprised by the facts and statistics, or whether they agree, disagree, or can identify with the quotes.

There are also definitions for difficult words or phrases which are important to understand a text which appears on the same page. (Words or phrases in the text are highlighted in **bold**.)

Vocabulary

Students meet a large amount of vocabulary during the course. It is important to encourage good learning skills from the start, for example:
● organizing vocabulary into categories rather than simple alphabetical lists
● understanding the context of vocabulary and whether it is a key word needed for production or for comprehension
● checking and learning the pronunciation of a word or phrase.

Language spot

This focuses on the grammar that is generated by the topic of the unit and concentrates on its practical application.

If your students need revision after completing the Language spot, direct them to the Grammar reference, which provides a handy check.

There is also one photocopiable Grammar test for each unit in this Teacher's Resource Book.

Listening, Reading, Speaking, Writing

These activities give realistic and communicative practice of language skills needed in commerce.

● In the listening activities students are exposed to business situations, including dialogues, presentations, and interviews. They also hear a variety of English accents, both native-speaker and non-native speaker.

● In the reading sections students meet a variety of business-based texts.

● In the speaking sections, try to ensure use of English during speaking activities, particularly those involving some discussion. Encourage this by teaching or revising any functional language students may need. The photocopiable activities in this Teacher's Resource Book also provide additional, freer discussion activities.

● Writing practice in the units is designed as consolidation of the topic with structured, meaningful writing tasks (see Writing bank).

Pronunciation

This practises aspects of pronunciation which are of maximum importance for intelligibility.

You can repeat the recordings in the Pronunciation as often as you like until you and your students to feel confident they have mastered a particular sound or feature.

Checklist

This allows students to check their own progress. You may want to get students to grade or assess how well they can perform each of the 'Can do' statements, e.g. 'easily', 'with difficulty', or 'not at all'.

Key words

These are the main items of commerce vocabulary introduced in the unit. A definition of each of these words appears in the Glossary. You should certainly check students' pronunciation, including the stress, of words likely to be used orally.

This section also provides students with the opportunity to personalize the Key words by adding five more words or expressions that they think are useful.

Writing bank

This is in the middle of the book and gives specific skills practice in basic business writing. It can be used throughout the course, either in class, or as self-study or homework. There are recommendations for when to use the different exercises in the teaching notes in this Teacher's Resource Book. There is also an Answer key in the Student's Book to encourage students to check their work, but it is important for you to check extended written answers with reference to the models provided.

Speaking activities

This section contains one or more parts of the information gap activities from the main units (see Speaking).

Grammar reference

This can be used together with the Language spot, as a handy check, or for revision. It shows the form of a particular grammar point, briefly explains its use, and provides example sentences as well as indicating likely student errors.

Listening scripts

This is a complete transcript of all the recordings. Direct students to it for checking answers after they have completed a Listening task, or allow weaker students to read it as they listen to a particular recording, perhaps for a final time.

Glossary

This is an alphabetical list of all the Key words. Each word is followed by the pronunciation in phonetic script, the part of speech, and a definition in English.

The section begins with a phonetic chart, with an example word from commerce to illustrate each of the sounds.

1 The business environment

Background

Every day millions of people all over the world are involved in business activities. They may be working for large international organizations with thousands of employees and business interests in many countries, or for a local business with a small workforce. These businesses may produce or sell goods, or they may provide services, such as tourism, medical care, or education. And even the people who aren't working are still involved in the business world as consumers. Every purchase they make, every text message they send, helps a business achieve its prime goal of making a profit.

Some businesses provide the goods and services that we all need to survive – food, water, shelter, clothes, and warmth. These five basic **needs** exist in all societies, from the most advanced to the least developed. In more developed societies, we let other people provide for most of our needs in exchange for payment. For example, we rely on other people to produce bread which arrives on our table through a series of financial transactions involving farmers, merchants, millers, bakers, and retailers. People in business provide the goods which other people need in return for profit. This in its turn enables them to pay for their own needs. The whole business world is interconnected in this way.

Other businesses provide the goods and services that we don't *need*, but *prefer* to have, such as home entertainment products and leisure travel services. These extra items reflect our desires or **wants**. Other wants include computers with ever-increasing capabilities and the latest mobile phones. Modern economies depend on these wants continually increasing. And as they increase, so more employees with specialized skills are needed, and millions of new jobs are created.

The growth of the Internet is having an enormous impact on the way we buy goods and services. In fact, in 2005 UK consumers spent nearly as much on goods online (£8.2 billion) as in high-street department stores (£9.4 billion).

✳ Tip

don't mind
Use this expression to say you don't feel uncomfortable or unhappy with something.

actually
In spoken English, when you disagree with a statement you can add *actually* to emphasize the contrast.

➕ Additional activity

(stronger students)
In exercise 3 students cover the text about Markus after reading it. They then ask and answer questions from the questionnaire from memory.

➕ Grammar test

Go to p. 68 Teacher's Resource Book.

Start up

1 Get students to do the questionnaire on their own.

2 Try the example dialogue with some students, then get them to work in pairs. Ask students to discuss what jobs would suit their work style.

3 Ask students to read about Markus. Ask some questions from the questionnaire, e. g. *Does Markus like travelling?* (Yes, he does.) Then get students to continue in pairs. Ask students what they think an exhibition organizer does. Ask them to read about Chloe, then ask some questions from the questionnaire, e.g. *Does Chloe enjoy teamwork?* (Yes, she does.) Tell students to continue in pairs..

⚷	1 M ✗ C ✓	2 M ? (probably) C ✓	3 M ? C ?	4 M ✓ C ?
	5 M ? C ?	6 M ✓ C ✓	7 M ? C ✗	8 M ✓ C ? (probably)
	9 M ? C ✗	10 M ? C ?	11 M ? C ?	12 M ✗ C ✗

Language spot
Present Simple

Go through the Present Simple with the students. Elicit the use of -*s* for third person and *do / does / don't / doesn't* for questions, negatives, and short answers. Get students to underline the sentences about Markus (*I work ... I travel ... I love ... I spend ... I enjoy ... I don't really like ... I get back ... it needs ...*).

Go through the rule about the *–ing* form. Get students to underline the sentences in the text about Chloe (*I love working ..., I like dealing with ..., I enjoy working ..., I hate dealing with ...*). In pairs, get students to tell each other about things they *enjoy / love / hate / are (not) good at*.

Go through the Grammar reference with students or set it as homework.

1 Go through the activity with the class. Elicit two or three duties for each job. Then get students to write sentences.

2 Get students to compare their answers.

3 If necessary do this orally first, then get the students to write their sentences.

> 1 George likes working in a team, but he doesn't like doing routine activities.
> 2 Stephanie likes dealing with people, but she doesn't like dealing with money.
> 3 Lauren likes doing research, but she doesn't like solving problems.
> 4 Andy likes using technology, but he doesn't like being creative.
> 5 Rachel likes meeting new people, but she doesn't like working under pressure.

Vocabulary

Ask students to record new words in a vocabulary notebook.

> organizer   operator   researcher   trainer   designer   controller   manager

Reading

1 Divide the students into small groups to discuss the questions.

2 Before reading, go through the questions and get students to guess the answers. Then get them to read the article and check their guesses.

> 1 About an hour and a half   2 Gossiping   3 26 minutes   4 40%
> 5 They use filters to prevent surfing, turn off coffee machines, and suspend workers.   6 They have rooms where staff can relax.

3 Divide the students into pairs to discuss the questions.

Listening

1 🎧 Go through the list, then play the recording for students to tick the activities.

> send emails, surf the Net, have meetings, speak to customers, fill in time sheets, key in data, send faxes, gossip, make coffee

2 🎧 Go through the questions with the students. Ask them if they remember the answers. Play the recording again and get them to write T or F.

> 1 T   2 F   3 T   4 F   5 F   6 T

✳ Tip

gossip
to talk informally about other people and their private lives

doodle
to draw lines, patterns, etc. without thinking, especially when you are bored

flirt
to behave or talk in a way that suggests you find someone attractive

✳ Tip

absenteeism
a situation where staff regularly have time off for illness. Here, the expression 'absenteeism in the workplace' suggests that staff are 'absent' when they are working on personal business.

suspended
not allowed to come into work for a period of time, as a punishment

* Tip

Top margin

Look at the statistic. Ask students why companies lose money when their staff surf the Net. (Because they do less work but still have to be paid.)

Company profile

Amazon.com

1 Get the students to discuss the questions in pairs.

2 Ask students to tell you what they know about Amazon.com. Ask each pair to decide who is Student A and Student B (whose information is on p.112). Students may note down key information. Then they cover the information and ask the questions.

> **Student A** 1 Over 5,000 2 Tailored services, product reviews, secure payment system, opportunity to 'look inside' books 3 With its powerful database 4 It once offered pocket computers for £7 instead of £192.
>
> **Student B** 1 A website where people can buy a wide range of goods 2 Products and services including books, CDs, DVDs, computer games, clothes, computers, mobile phones, cameras, travel services 3 Tens of millions of items 4 In Seattle, in the United States 5 Six

3 Ask students to find the terms and translate them.

Project

1 Go through the instructions and example. Ask pairs to think of a famous company and write questions they would like to find the answers to.

2 Tell students that their answers should be short like the example.

Get students to go online and find the answers (start by searching for 'company information' or 'company profiles').

☐ Additional activity

(stronger students)

Students do an oral presentation of their project. They can ask the class to guess the answers to the questions before they tell them.

Vocabulary

1 Get students to discuss how to say the numbers.

2 ⌒ Make sure your students know how to say large numbers and fractions. Get students to write down the numbers, then play the recording and get students to check and correct the numbers.

> 1 Five hundred and thirteen; Two thousand, eight hundred and ninety-two; Two thirds; Nine point five six
>
> 2 1 Two hundred and fifty; Five thousand, seven hundred and eighty-nine; 2 A half; Three quarters; A third; 3 Three point five; Fifteen point oh six; Seven point nine six

* Tip

Saying numbers

Say 'and' after hundreds and between thousands and tens

480 *four hundred and eighty*

1,018 *one thousand and eighteen*

per cent

Say the number and then 'per cent'

53% *fifty-three per cent*

decimals

Say 'point' after the whole number and say the numbers after the point separately

4.73 *four point seven three*

fractions

½ *a half*, ⅔ *two thirds*, ¼ *a quarter*

☐ Additional activity

(weaker students)

Dictate these numbers to students. They can write numerals.

155 58,670 3,790 317 690 377 8,237

Pronunciation

Numbers

1 ⌒ Play the recording and get students to circle the numbers they hear.

> 1 a 150,000   b 90   c 50   d 13.5   e 14   f 2,317

2 Students do the exercise in pairs. Go over common errors at class level.

➕ Photocopiable activity
Introducing yourself
Go to p.69 Teacher's Resource Book.

9 to 5

Meeting people

1 Get students to guess who the people are and what they are saying.

2 🎧 Play the recording and check.

3 🎧 Get students to guess who says what then listen and check. Ask students to translate the expressions in their vocabulary books.

> 🔑 1 S 2 R 3 R 4 R 5 R 6 S 7 L

4 🎧 Play the final part of the conversation. Discuss the answer at class level.

> 🔑 4 Joe recognizes her. They go to the same gym.

➕ Additional activity
(stronger students)
Ask students to invent new identities and swap roles if necessary.

➕ Additional activity
(weaker students)
Ask students to write out one dialogue for homework.

Speaking

Go through the *Expressions* list with students. Ask them to repeat the sentences after you or after the recording.

Tell students to decide what role they will each play, and to read through their *Speaking activities*. Remind them to refer to the *Expressions* list during this activity and to say *Sorry. Have you got a moment?*

After a short time, interrupt and ask a strong group to perform the dialogue, helping them where necessary. Then ask all groups to try the task again.

✳ Tip
Top margin
Ask students if they agree or disagree with Keiko and Enrique. Ask them what other things they think you need to get a job in business.

Business know-how

1 Ask students to read the tips and choose the three most helpful ones.

2 Students discuss the advice and add ideas, e.g. talk to people working in business, research online, get a language qualification, improve your computer skills, etc.

➕ Additional activity
(stronger students)
Students can add another paragraph to the letter: *I like ... I hate ... I'm good at ... I'm not good at ...*

➕ Writing bank
Emails 1
Go to p. 52 Student's Book.

Writing

Depending on their situation, ask students to think about a job from the unit or talk about the job they are doing.

Checklist

Go through the checklist with the students. Get them to tell you which activities in the unit helped them practise each point. Ask students to tick the points they feel they can perform. Ask the class if they need more practice in any of the areas.

Key words

Go through the list of words to check students' understanding.

2 The company

Background

Self-employed people have to do everything themselves. A plumber, for example, has to buy his own tools and equipment, carry out the work himself, decide how to advertise his business, and fix his own price scales. If he needed to raise capital for a business investment (such as a new van), he would arrange a loan from the bank. He would also do his own book-keeping and, possibly, his own tax declarations. He may decide to take on an assistant to lighten his workload. However, as companies expand and more people are employed, one person can no longer perform all the administrative and decision-making functions. Organization, and the division of labour, is required.

In larger businesses, there must be people who can take authority for certain decisions and who can tell other employees what to do. A typical chain of command would start with the Chairman at the top, then the Chief Executive, followed by (in large organizations) the heads of divisions (such as the Group Finance Director), then the heads of departments (such as Sales and Marketing, Human Resources, Finance, etc.), and finally the people who work in the office or on the shop floor.

Every person in an organization is a member of a formal group within which he or she has to perform specific tasks. This breakdown of an organization into formal groups offers a number of advantages: workers specializing in specific areas can perform more effectively, which reduces company costs; there is a clear chain of command as employees receive instructions from their line manager; the employees' performance can be monitored more easily; and there is better internal communication as managers can speak for the section they control. At the same time, employees can experience the benefits of working in a team, and they can also ask their supervisor or more experienced colleagues for help and guidance.

Of course, a departmental organization can also have certain disadvantages: some employees may be so focused on their own particular tasks that they become cut off from employees in other departments; and managers may be more concerned with their own and their department's performance than with the overall performance of the company.

Start up

In pairs, students brainstorm as many roles as necessary. They don't need to know the name of the job, but they have to think about what jobs are needed to develop and produce a product.

> **O─ Possible answers**
> You need people to make the product, research it, design it, promote it, keep the computers working, manage the offices and factories, manage the money and budgets, write letters and emails, etc.

* Tip

billing
preparing and sending bills to customers
salary
the money a person gets for a job
tax
part of your income that you pay to the government
investment
putting money in a bank, business or property in order to make a profit
recruiting
finding new staff to join a company
maintenance
keeping a building in good condition

Vocabulary

1 Ask students to look at the picture in pairs. Ask them to say which department they think the people work in.

2 Go through the descriptions with the students.

Get students to match the departments with the descriptions.

> **O─** 2 G   3 F   4 B   5 A   6 C   7 E

✚ Photocopiable activity
Departments
Go to p.71 Teacher's Resource Book.

✚ Additional activity
(weaker students)
Write *Harun / accounts clerk / salaries* on the board. Dictate the text to your students. Ask them: *What does Harun do? What is he doing at the moment?*

> My name's Harun. I work in the Finance department of a mobile phone company. I'm an accounts clerk. We're getting the salaries ready for the end of the month. It's always busy at this time.

✚ Additional activity
(stronger students)
Read out the text about Harun and get students to make notes. Then get students to ask each other questions, for example *What does Harun do? What sort of company does he work for? What's he doing at the moment?*

✚ Grammar test
Go to p.70 Teacher's Resource Book.

∗ Tip
Top margin
Read the top margin e-words with the students. Point out that new terms like these are being created all the time.
e-books books that exist only electronically, and have to be downloaded
e-business business done on the Internet
e-cards greetings cards that are sent by email
e-market an internet site where you can display services and goods. No actual trade takes place on these sites.
e-museum a collection of documents, archives, etc. available in an electronic form
e-ticket a ticket that is created electronically and that you print out yourself

Listening

1 🎧 Ask students what departments Montse and Kenichiro work in (Human Resources and Purchasing) and what they working on at the moment (a job advert and buying for next year's spring season).

Ask students to read the article and try to guess the missing words. Play the recording and ask them to complete the gaps. Play the recording as often as necessary.

> ⌐🔑 1 helping   2 copy   3 get   4 checks   5 training   6 everything
> 7 team   8 learn   9 currently   10 colours

2 Get students to discuss which job they would prefer.

Language spot
Present Simple v Present Continuous

Ask students to read the language rules and write 'Present Continuous' and 'Present Simple' in the correct places ('Present Simple' is first). Get them to underline examples of the two tenses in the article (Present Simple: *My manager checks ... I work ...* Present Continuous: *I'm training ... I'm helping ... I'm writing ... I'm doing ... I'm working ... I'm enjoying ... We're currently buying ...*)

Go through the Grammar reference with students or set it as homework.

Ask students to complete the letter in class or as homework.

> ⌐🔑 2 'm having   3 'm writing   4 'm working   5 'm improving
> 6 'm learning   7 'm not staying   8 's   9 exports   10 'm working
> 11 finish   12 'm having / have   13 eat   14 go   15 spend

Reading

1 Get students to read the introduction and discuss how we use the Internet in business.

> ⌐🔑 **Possible answers**
> buying products and services, finding information, booking hotels, sending documents, sharing data, placing orders, making payments, doing market research, keeping in contact with clients, etc.

2 Ask students to read the article and ask them these questions:

What is e-commerce? (buying and selling over the Internet)
How many types of e-commerce are there? (three types)
What are they called? (B2C / Business to Consumer, C2C / Consumer to Consumer, B2B / Business to Business)
Which type does Ford use to cut costs? (B2B)
Which part of the world is most e-active? (Europe)

Get students to find the words and match them with the definitions.

> ⌐🔑 2 d   3 b   4 e   5 a

3 Ask students to read the article again and do the exercise.

🔑 1 F   2 T   3 F   4 F   5 T   6 F

4 Set this exercise in class or for homework.

🔑 1 costs   2 order   3 bid   4 supplier   5 Purchasing

5 Put the students in groups. Get them to brainstorm the advantages and disadvantages of e-commerce.

> 🔑 **Possible answers**
> **Advantages:** A small business can reach as many clients as a large one; It saves money; It is more efficient; Companies can respond immediately to customer enquiries; Customers can visit a website at any time of the day, etc.
> **Disadvantages:** It can need a lot of staff to manage it; It can cause time-wasting enquiries; Consumers may worry about sending credit card details; Customers may not know whether the company is reliable, etc.

Pronunciation
Phone numbers

1 🎧 Play the recording and get students to listen and repeat the numbers.

2 🎧 Get students to listen again and answer the questions.

> 🔑 1 use 'double', e.g. 'double eight'   2 'oh' and 'zero'   3 pause after the first three numbers, e.g. 'five five two, six four seven'

3 Get students to dictate numbers in pairs.

Call centre
Making a call

🎧 Ask students to read the dialogue in pairs and guess what words are missing. Play the recording and get students to complete the gaps.

Go through *Expressions* with the students.

> 🔑 1 can   2 speak   3 moment   4 that   5 this   6 office
> 7 out   8 number

Speaking

Get students to read their *Speaking activities* and role-play the phone conversations, referring to the *Expressions* list.

After the first dialogue, interrupt the students and ask a strong group to perform the dialogue, helping them where necessary.

It's my job

1 Get students to discuss the questions in pairs.

2 Ask students to read about Daniel and answer the questions.

➕ Additional activity
(weaker students)
Dictate these numbers to the students.
1 01876 542290
2 02087 661003

➕ Additional activity
(stronger students)
In pairs, get students to dictate numbers to each other.

✳ Tip
Top margin
Ask students to read the information. Discuss these questions:
● Have you ever received calls at home from call centres?
● Do you think it is an effective way to sell?
● Why did you last a call centre?

3 Get the students to discuss the questions in pairs.

Business know-how

1 Get students to discuss the questions in pairs or groups.

2 Ask students to read *Business know-how* and discuss the suggestions. Write students' tips on the blackboard and ask students to choose the two most useful.

Writing

1 Get students to read the web page and answer the questions.

2 Students write a web page for their own company or school.

Project

Orange is a successful mobile phone company. We suggest using their UK site for this exercise. For a description of the company departments go to **Orange Careers**, then click on **the company**. There are links to **call centres**, **technical**, **retail**, **professional**. Put those four links on the board and ask students to use them as headings for making notes.

Checklist

Go through the checklist with the students. Get them to tell you which activities in the unit helped them practise each point. Ask students to tick the points they feel they can perform. Ask the class if they need more practice in any of the areas.

Key words

Go through the list of words to check students' understanding.

✳ Tip

deadline
a date or time by which you have to complete a task
prioritize
to put several tasks in order of importance

✚ Additional activity

(stronger students)
On the Orange site, encourage students to look at some of the employee profiles. Tell them they don't need to understand every word, just get the general gist.

✚ Additional activity

(weaker students)
Get students to find the four links: **call centres**, **technical**, **retail**, **professional**. Then ask them to click on **What could I do?** They can then write down three or four job titles for each heading.

3 Travel

Background

We are travelling more and more. In the UK alone, the number of flight passengers increased from 70 million in 2000 to 80 million in 2004. Budget airlines have had an enormous impact, and this growth is expected to continue.

In the UK, 1.5 million people (out of a working population of 26 million) work in travel and tourism. It is a major industry with many different sectors including:

- airlines
- hotels
- transportation (train and coach travel, car hire, etc.)
- food services
- corporate travel services
- travel agents and tour operators.

Tourism is similar to a manufacturing industry, with different components (hotel rooms, flights, meals, trips, etc.) bought and assembled by tour operators to produce holidays. Travel agents then sell these products to the public, while representatives of the tour operator provide an after-sales service to the consumer. The larger the tour operator, the more specialized the role of each employee, with jobs in marketing, research and development, negotiating with couriers, etc.

A 2005 survey of US employees revealed that 48% of the interviewees were travelling less frequently for work than in 2000. However, while many companies are cutting down on travel, it remains a major factor in business expenses and in the wider world of the travel industry. In the USA, 18% of the total number of journeys taken are business-related. These business trips break down into the following categories:

- 44% are for general business purposes such as meetings, consulting, etc.
- 22% are for attending conferences or seminars
- 34% are for business and pleasure combined
- 32% of all business trips involve flights.

When travelling on business, it is always a good idea to check your bill. The average corporate traveller in the USA is overcharged $11.35 a night, while American businesses pay more then $1.8 million on excess charges every day. But we find it hard to leave the office behind – another survey suggested that 43% of business people stayed in contact with their offices via email – even when they were on holiday!

➕ Additional activity

(all levels)
Before Start up, tell students about a difficult journey you had. Instead of asking them comprehension questions, get them to write and then ask five questions about your story.

➕ Additional activity

(all levels)
Get students to write up their story for homework.

Start up

1 Get students to look quickly at the titles and pictures and guess what they think each story will be about. Then ask them to read the stories and choose the answers.

🔑 1 C 2 D 3 A 4 B

2 Get students to decide which is the worst, funniest, etc. story.

3 Ask students to think individually about a difficult journey they have had, and to make notes. Write these expressions from the article on the board.

Starting the story: *Last year / month ...   About a month / Two years ago ...*
Joining ideas: *and / because / but / However, ... / Unfortunately, ...*
Commenting and concluding:
It didn't make a good impression.   What a disaster!
There was nothing I could do.   It was a nightmare.

Get students to tell their stories in groups, using the Past Simple.

➕ Grammar test
Go to p.72 Teacher's Resource Book.

Language spot
Past Simple

Get students to read through the rules. Elicit from students how you form the regular Past Simple and ask them to find examples in the article (*stopped, arrived, decided, booked, arranged, checked in, realized, tried*). Elicit how you form the negative and find examples in the article (*couldn't call, didn't make, didn't have, didn't accept*). Then get students to underline the irregular verbs in the article. Ask them to write the base forms of the verbs.

Go through the Grammar reference with students or set it as homework.

> **O━** was (be)   took (take)   had (have)   got (get)   flew (fly)   found (find)

Get students to write sentences about Jack's trip.

> **O━** 1 He arrived at the airport at 7.30 a.m.   2 He checked in at zone B.
> 3 He went through security and passport control at 8.00 a.m.
> 4 He waited in the departure lounge for an hour.   5 He went to gate 16 to board the plane.   6 The plane / he took off at 9.45 a.m.
> 7 It / he landed in Madrid.

➕ Photocopiable activity
Greeting visitors
Go to p.73 Teacher's Resource Book.

Vocabulary

1 Before doing the exercise, get students to tell you what happens in each part of the airport. Then get them to match them with the explanations.

> **O━** 1 d   2 f   3 g   4 b   5 a   6 c   7 e

2 Ask students to tick the things they did the last time they travelled abroad. Go through answers, making sure students say them in the Past Simple.

3 Encourage students to have a general conversation about travel. Go through common errors or difficulties afterwards.

9 to 5
Apologizing

1 Ask students to look at the pictures and guess what is happening.

2 🎧 Get students to focus on picture 1. Play the recording. As they listen, they number the events in order. Ask what Lisa did last night.

> **O━** caught a bus = 4   ran to the office = 6   missed a train = 2
> went to bed late = 1   waited in a traffic jam = 5   tried to get a taxi = 3

3 🎧 Get students to focus on picture 2. Play the recording and get students to tick the expressions they hear. Ask students: *What is Richard's reaction to Lisa's apology? What is happening at 8 a.m. tomorrow?*

> **O━** I'm so sorry ...   Don't worry about it.   I promise ...
> I feel really bad about it.   It'll never happen again.   That's OK.

Speaking

Go through the *Expressions* list, asking students to repeat after you.

Tell students to read through their *Speaking activities* and make notes. (Both activities involve people in work situations who have to apologize for being late and explain what happened.) Students then role-play the conversations, referring to the *Expressions* list during the activity.

Ask stronger pairs to perform their dialogue.

✱ Tip

Top margin
Brainstorm with students what you get in a three-star hotel. Ask students to check their guesses with the text.

➕ Additional activity

(all levels)
Ask students to think of a two large hotels in their town or city. Get them to look the hotels up on the Internet and complete reviews of them as in exercise 2.

➕ Additional activity

(stronger students)
Tell students that they are going to go to a conference in London. Tell them to decide what level of hotel they want, and what facilities. Get them to research a hotel online and find a suitable hotel.

Reading

1 Ask students: *What are the main things you expect from a good hotel?* Ask them where the ads are and what sort of traveller they are aimed at. Pre-teach: **hairdryer**, **wireless**, **en suite**, **trouser press**, and **on-site parking**. Ask them to read the ads and answer the questions.

O⚊ 1 A 2 C 3 B 4 B 5 C

2 Ask students to complete the internet review.

O⚊	Arena	Shamrock	Paradise
en suite rooms	✓	✓	✗
non-smoking rooms	✓	✗	✗
continental and Irish breakfast	✗	✗	✓
direct-dial phones	✓	✗	✓
internet access in bedrooms	✗	✓	✓
TV	✓	✓	✓
hairdryer	✓	✓	✓
trouser press	✗	✓	✗
minibar	✓	✗	✗
restaurant	✗	✓	✗
free car-parking	✓	✗	✓
conference facilities	✓	✗	✓

3 In pairs, get students to list the five most important qualities for a business hotel. Get some pairs to present their answers to the class.

Speaking

Tell students to take time to read through the information – one student is a customer calling the hotel and the other is a hotel receptionist. Remind them of the expressions for apologizing in the previous unit.

After the first role-play, interrupt and ask a strong group to perform the dialogue, helping them where necessary.

* Tip

Top margin
- Read the definition of **transport**. Brainstorm with students different forms of transport.
- Read the statistics with students. Ask them to compare this to their country. What are the positive and negative results of this change in the amount we travel?

* Tip

base the main place a company does it business from

carrier a company which takes people or goods from one place to another

➕ Writing bank
Emails 2 – Hotel booking
Go to p.53 Student's Book.

Company profile

bmi

1 Ask students to discuss the points in pairs. Then round up students' ideas on the board.

2 Get students to read *Company profile* and match the questions.

> **Oⅎ** 1 F 2 D 3 C 4 A 5 G 6 B 7 E

3 Ask students to find the words and translate them in their notebooks.

> **Oⅎ** 1 share 2 losses 3 profit 4 awards 5 punctual

Project

1 Get students to work in pairs or groups to do the research. Ask them to use the questions in *Company profile* 2 as headings for their notes.

2 Get students to write their report in the form of questions and answers.

Business know-how

1 In pairs, get students to discuss the questions. Round up their answers.

2 Ask students to discuss which tips they like best, and to add two more. Round up ideas on the board.

Writing

Ask students to read the email. Ask who it's from, who it's to, and what it's about. What does John want Richard to do? Get students to make a list of the things Richard has to do, then complete the internet form.

> **Oⅎ** **Check-in date**: 14 April; **Check-out date**: 16 April; **No. of rooms**: 1; **No. of nights**: 2; **Guests per room**: 1; double-sole occupancy; non-smoking; **Beds**: double; **Title**: Mr; **First name**: John; **Surname**: Conrad; **No. of house**: 156; **Street name**: Buzan Road; **Town / City**: Manchester; **County / State**: blank; **Postcode / Zipcode**: M3 2PB; **Country**: UK; **Tel. no.**: 0161 9625494; **Email address**: john.conrad@perfectworld.com

Checklist

Go through the checklist with the students. Get them to tell you which activities in the unit helped them practise each point. Ask students to tick the points they feel they can perform. Ask the class if they need more practice in any of the areas.

Key words

Go through the list of words to check students' understanding.

4 Sport

Background

Sport is big business. It features some of the world's biggest celebrities; it attracts major sponsorship deals; it produces great sporting events from the Super Bowl to the Olympics; and it has billions of followers worldwide. In the UK, the sports sector employs half a million people. It also accounts for more than 2% of the UK gross domestic product and about 3% of consumer expenditure.

One visible example of business in sport is sponsorship. Athletes promote a particular brand of running shoes, well-known teams always have the logo of a sportswear manufacturer on show, and famous companies pay huge sums of money to have their name on the shirts of top football clubs. Some sporting events and teams even adopt the name of their sponsor.

Sponsorship can have several benefits for the sponsor: it brings its name to the attention of the public, enables the company to reduce its tax bill, and enhances its image. For sport, it generates extra income, raising the standard of the team or club, and enhances the status of the team.

However, there can be disadvantages, too. The sponsor may suffer if it doesn't receive sufficient publicity, if the sport develops a bad image, or if the sponsor is associated with a losing team. And it may be problematic for sport if it becomes too dependent on sponsorship money. And while major sports such as football may thrive, minor sports may not attract sponsors and extra income.

There are a wide variety of careers in sport – even for people who can't kick a ball! Some of the main areas are:

- Sporting goods – sports clothes have become the global leisure wear of choice. The sector involves manufacturers, designers, suppliers, retailers, etc.
- Health and fitness – this is a steadily growing sector. Professionals include aerobics instructors, personal trainers, etc.
- Sports media – this includes all jobs involved in sports coverage in newspapers, TV and radio, and on the Internet.
- Sports venues – from golf courses to huge stadiums, there are careers for in-house teams (managers, administrators, etc.) and for external suppliers.
- Sports events – major events such as the World Cup need large staffs to manage them. Event management involves marketing, sales, client services, public relations, etc.
- Professional services – these include sports law specialists, accountants, players' agents, etc.

Start up

Look at the photos with the students and ask them what the sports are. Discuss the questions with the class.

Listening 1

1 🎧 Play the recording and get students to identify the sports. Ask them what the words and expressions were that helped them to guess.

🔑 1 windsurfing 2 fencing

2 🎧 Play the recording again to find out why the people enjoy the sports.

🔑 1 loves speed and being on the water
2 it's quick, competitive, and romantic

3 In pairs, get students to ask and answer the questions in the questionnaire. Discuss the answers at class level.

Reading

1 In groups, get students to brainstorm industries associated with sport.

2 Ask students to read the article and add industries and jobs to their lists.

3 Ask them to read the article again and match headings with paragraphs.

> ⚷ Sponsorship = 5   The media = 6   Event organization and tickets = 3
> Location = 2   Clothing and equipment = 4   Education and training = 1

4 Get students to do the exercise and write the expressions in their vocabulary notebook.

> ⚷ a wide range of careers   a major leisure industry
> substantial investment   significant business   enormous profits

5 In pairs, get students to discuss the question. Then ask the class if anyone would like to work in the sports industry.

Language spot
Present Perfect

Ask students to read and complete the rules. Go through the Grammar reference with students or set it as homework.

> ⚷ When we talk *in general* about ... that have a *result* in the present. ... when we talk *in detail* about ...

1 Ask students to answer the questions individually.

2 In pairs, get students to ask and answer the questions. Point out that the second question asks for specific details about the event so it uses the Past Simple.

3 Get students to do this exercise in class or at home.

> ⚷ 2 Have you ever sent an email to the wrong person? No, I haven't.
>   3 Have you ever travelled to a foreign country on business? Yes, I have. I travelled to Kenya six months ago.
>   4 Has your company ever sent you on a training course? No, it hasn't.
>   5 Have you ever booked a flight online? Yes, I have. I booked it / one yesterday.
>   6 Have you ever attended a conference? Yes, I have. I attended a conference in Tokyo in 2005.

4 Get students to complete the email.

> ⚷ 1 've made   2 've missed   3 've lost   4 was   5 forgot
>   6 downloaded   7 had   8 Have, eaten   9 felt   10 Have, had

---

Sidebar (left column)

✚ **Photocopiable activity**
Careers in sports
Go to p.75 Teacher's Resource Book.

✚ **Additional activity**
(all levels)
Ask students to find what these numbers refer to: 500,000, 3%, $1 billion, £50 million, $26 billion.

✚ **Grammar test**
Go to p.74 Teacher's Resource Book.

✱ **Tip**
With a weaker class, go through the email with the class before they do it individually. Explain that in the first paragraph (1–3) Emily is listing her experiences up to now and so they require the Present Perfect. In the second paragraph (4–7) Emily gives detail about when she did things, so it requires the Past Simple. Points 8 and 10 are questions about experiences and require the Present Perfect. Point 9 refers to a specific time in the past and requires the Past Simple. *With a stronger class*, ask students to explain why they have chosen the Present Perfect or the Past Simple in the email.

∗ Tip

Top margin
Ask students to read about summer camps. Ask them if they would like to work in a summer camp in the US.

➕ Additional activity

(weaker students)
Before getting students to do exercise 3, get them to ask you the questions. After the task get the students to write their own answers to the questions.

➕ Additional activity

(stronger students)
Swap pairs around. Get students to tell their new partner about their last partner's answers.

➕ Writing bank
Letters 1 – Thanking
Go to p.54 Student's Book.

Listening 2

1 Ask students: *What job opportunities are there for short term summer work in your country? Have you ever done any summer jobs?* Then get them to read about summer camps and answer the question.

2 🎧 Go through the form, then play the recording and ask students to complete it. Get them to check their answers in pairs and then listen again.

> ⊙━ Name: Jacek Gomulski   Date of birth: 15 May 1987
> Nationality: Polish   Education: University of Warsaw
> Have you ever worked or travelled in the United States?: Yes
> If so, why and when?: Holiday, last year
> Have you worked in a summer camp before?: No
> What sports can you do?: Football, basketball, tennis, swimming, sailing
> Have you got any relevant qualifications or experience?: Yes
> If so, what are they?: Taught sports at a summer school
> Can you drive?: Yes

3 In pairs, students take it in turns to be interviewer and job applicants. They can talk about their own experience or invent a new role.

Call centre

Leaving a message

1 🎧 Ask students: *Do you ever take phone messages? How do you pass the message on? Have you ever had a phone message that wasn't clear? What was the problem?* Play the recording and check the secretary's notes (He wrote 4.30, not 5.30).

2 🎧 Go through all the expressions with students, then play the recording again and get students to tick the expressions.

> ⊙━ Can I take a message?   Can you spell that, please?   Can I check that?
> OK, I'll give Tom the message.

3 🎧 Ask students to copy the message pad twice in their notebooks, leaving space for notes. Play the recording and ask students to make notes. Get them to work in pairs to compare their answers, and then play the recording again.

> ⊙━ 1 **Message for**: — ; **Message from**: Dave from IT; **Phone number**: extension 4677; **Message**: Delete all emails on computer from Klaus Trawoeger.
> 2 **Message for**: James Tate; **Message from**: Tina Winters from Ricchissimo Fashions; **Phone number**: — ; **Message**: Call Tina this afternoon.

Speaking

Go through the *Expressions* list, asking students to repeat after you.

Divide the class into pairs. Tell students to read through their *Speaking activities* – they will role-play a caller leaving a message with a secretary. Students should refer to the *Expressions* list during this activity.

After the first activity, interrupt the students and ask a strong pair to perform the dialogue, helping them where necessary. Then ask all the groups to try the second speaking task.

It's my job

1 Get students to discuss the questions.

2 Ask them to read the article and answer the questions.

> ⊙━ 1 Assistant Manager at a big leisure centre   2 good technical knowledge of running the business and facilities; be good at communicating with customers and the press   3 It's very varied.

✚ Additional activity
(stronger students)
After reading *It's my job*, ask students to read it again and then close their books. Write the beginnings of the sentences on the board: *I'm the …; It's got …; I started as …; But I trained in …; You need a …; You also have …; I like the fact that …; This morning I …; No two days …*
In groups, get students to listen to you reading the text, without taking notes, then try to recreate the text.

✚ Additional activity
(weaker students)
After reading *It's my job*, ask students to close their books. Then divide them into two groups and ask these questions. The first group to answer each question gets 10 points.
What does Ali do? What facilities has the leisure centre got? When did he start? What does he have to be good at in his job? What did he do in the morning and in the afternoon?

Project

In pairs, students think of the different brands for the four categories. Ask them to find out about sponsorship for one company from each category. Get them to write a report and / or give a presentation to the class.

Business know-how

1 Get students to discuss the questions in pairs.

2 Get students to decide which tips are useful, and add two more.

Writing

1 Go through the job ad with students. Ask if they have the qualifications for the job. Then ask them to complete the letter with the expressions.

2 Get students to write a letter of application using the letter as a model.

> ⊙━ 1 to apply for   2 relevant work experience   3 I believe
> 4 I am interested in   5 to meet with you

Checklist

Go through the checklist with students. Get them to tell you which activities in the unit helped them practise each point. Ask students if they need more practice in any of the areas.

Key words

Go through the list of words to check students' understanding.

5 Sales

Background

Business involves buying and selling. Customers, or buyers, want to buy a product or service; the sales person simply has to convince them that *this* product is the one they need. However, sales isn't simply about 'selling'. It involves relationships, psychology, attitude, ethics, information, and trust.

Some of the key concepts in sales are:

- **feature** – an aspect of the product or service. It could be its size, speed, colour, function, etc.
- **benefit** – this is what the customer gains from having the product or service. It may be tangible (cleaner clothes, faster travel, etc.) or intangible (convenience, enhanced social status, etc.). Customers don't buy features, they buy benefits.
- **active listening** – asking questions and actually listening to the customers' answers, finding out what they want and don't want, and understanding how they feel and what their issues are, is of vital importance to the sales person.
- **USPs** – these are 'unique selling points', the most valuable advantages that your product or service has over its rivals.
- **FABs** – or 'features, advantages, and benefits'. When presenting the product, these are the links between the product description, its advantage over rival products, and the gain that the customer has from using it.

But how do sales people actually achieve sales? Sales techniques are constantly developing. However, the traditional selling model which is still widely taught today is the Seven Steps of Selling:

1 **planning and preparation** know your product, know your market, know the competition, prepare your presentation
2 **opening** smile, be professional, explain the purpose of your visit, ask how long the prospective buyer has and if you can take notes
3 **questioning** to confirm or discover the major benefit(s) that the product / service will give the customer, and to build relationships
4 **presentation** focus on the unique benefit that the customer will get from the product, matching the benefits with the customer's needs, priorities, and motives
5 **overcoming objections** avoid argument and confrontation; understand the issues and then address them
6 **closing** the best close is short and sweet, all the key points having been covered
7 **after-sales follow-up** the completing of all the necessary paperwork, ongoing contact to make sure that the customer is happy and to resolve any problems

Start up

Get students to read the headlines and answer the questions. Discuss this as a class

O─ A 2 B 1 C 2 D 2 E 2 F 1 G 1 H 1

Vocabulary

1 Get students to read the headlines again and complete the table, then copy the words into their vocabulary notebooks.

| O─ | sales up | adjective = *rising* | noun = *rise* |
| | sales down | verbs = *to fall, to decrease* | noun = *fall* |

2 Divide students into groups and get them to talk about the different products from their own knowledge and experience. Ask them to justify their opinions. Round up at class level.

(all levels)

Before doing exercise 2, ask students to read the text and answer these questions about each paragraph:

A What is the difference between a benefit and a feature?

B What is a USP?

C If you are a new company, what should you do before you advertise?

D What should you let customers do first?

E Should a sales person talk a lot or listen a lot? Why?

F What sort of person should you sell to?

G How can you turn customers into sales people?

✱ Tip

USPs (Unique Selling Points)

These are the specific factors that differentiate one product or service from another. Some common types of USP are: unusual product features, good value for money, exceptional quality of service or quality of product, a famous name, easy availability.

➕ **Additional activity**

(weaker students)

Explain to students that the article is giving advice, and that this often involves the Imperative and Modals such as *must* and *need*. Ask students to go through the article and underline examples of these forms.

➕ **Photocopiable activity**

Needs, wants and preferences

Go to p.77 Teacher's Resource Book.

Reading

1 In pairs, get students to consider their buying style by discussing the questions.

2 Ask students to look at the article on p.29 and guess what it is about. Ask students to read the article and find the information in the text to justify their answers to the questions.

> ⊶ 2 E – Sell benefits not features   3 E – Differentiate your product
> 4 NE – Learn to listen   5 E – Learn to listen   6 E – Sell to people who buy

3 Ask students to read the text again and find the words and expressions.

> ⊶ 1 features   2 differentiate   3 direct mailing   4 jump to conclusions
> 5 superior to   6 word of mouth

4 In pairs, get students to invent a product. Ask them to do a simple drawing, give it a name, and decide on its benefits and USPs. Encourage them to be as creative as possible by asking them to brainstorm what features they would like the product to have, e.g. *I would like my computer to tell me that it is developing a problem before it actually stops working, like a person says they feel ill before they go to bed for a week!*

5 Ask the pairs to find another pair near them and to try and sell their product. Remind them to use the techniques from the article.

9 to 5

Invitations

1 Ask students to speculate about the pictures. Picture 1: *What do you think Joe and Lisa are doing?* Picture 2: *What do you think Joe is asking Lisa?*

2 🎧 Ask students to focus on Picture 1. Play the recording and get students to answer the questions.

> ⊶ 1 To see him about his PowerPoint presentation
> 2 Yes, at a breakfast meeting the next day

3 🎧 Play the recording again and get students to complete the diary.

> ⊶ **Monday**
> 2.00   meet the Marketing Director
> 3.15   make a call
> 3.30   go to sales meeting
> **Tuesday**
> 8.30   meet Joe
> 10.30   talk to the

4 🎧 Ask students to focus on Picture 2. Play the recording and get them to answer the questions.

O— 1 To go for a drink
2 She's taking her sister shopping.
3 She's going out with some university friends.
4 There's a Coldplay concert.
5 Yes

Go through the *Expressions*. Get students to repeat them after you or after the recording, then copy them into their notebook.

Language spot
Present Continuous for future, *be going to*

Ask students to read the rules for the Present Continuous and *be going to*, and complete the examples. Go through the Grammar reference with the students or set it as homework.

O— I'm *meeting* Clare for dinner tomorrow evening.
We're leaving for Madrid *tomorrow*.
Who *are* you *going to call* this afternoon?
I'm tired! I'm *going to* turn off my computer and go home.
DVD sales *are going to increase*.

1 Ask students to complete the dialogue.

O— 1 're having   2 is, arriving   3 're briefing   4 's happening
5 're preparing   6 're attending   7 're presenting   8 Am, seeing
9 aren't / 're not   10 're calling   11 Am, doing   12 're having

2 In pairs, get students to discuss the things they have planned.

3 In class or for homework, get students to write sentences about Holly.

Pronunciation
going to

1 ♪ Play the recording and ask students to read the sentences as they listen. Discuss with them the use of the shortened 'to'. Point out that in pop songs they often hear and read 'gonna'.

2 ♪ Play the sentences one at a time and get students to listen and repeat. Then in pairs get students to practise saying the sentences. Then play the recording again so they can check their performance.

Speaking

Divide the class into groups of three. Tell students to read their *Speaking activities*, which contain a task and a diary.

Go round the groups checking their progress. If necessary, interrupt the activity and deal with common errors before letting the students continue.

✱ Tip
Top margin
Ask students to work in pairs and explain in their own words what the quotes mean.
1st quote: Good organization results in more action than talking.
2nd quote: The result of a meeting should be action. If you have to have another meeting, the first one wasn't successful.
outcome result
lousy *(slang)* very bad
3rd quote: Meetings involve many different people giving their opinions, and this often wastes time and complicates things.
Ask students to think of the positive side to having meetings.

✚ Grammar test
Go to p.76 Teacher's Resource Book.

✱ Tip
Before studying the grammar rules, go to the Listening script on p.123 and get students to underline examples of the Present Continuous. There are a lot of examples because Lisa and Joe are talking about arrangements and fixed plans, often with another person.
Ask them to circle the one example of *be going to*. Ask: *Why doesn't Lisa use the Present Continuous?* (Because it is a prediction about the sales meeting.)

✚ Additional activity
(weaker students)
After exercise 2 get students to write a series of sentences about their plans and their partner's plans.

✚ Additional activity

(all levels)

Get students to write three USPs for their partner, e.g. *Giovanni is very passionate about the things that interest him, such as his city.*

Then they show them to their partner and discuss them.

✚ Writing bank
Emails 3 – Arranging a meeting
Go to p.55 Student's Book.

✱ Tip

auction *(noun)* a public meeting where property is sold to the person who offers the most money
auction *(verb)* to offer something for sale at an auction
turnover the value of goods or services a company sells in a period of time
transaction an occasion when something is bought
delivery taking goods to a customer
merge to join together

✚ Additional activity

(stronger students)

Instead of giving students questions to use in their research, ask them to write a series of questions that they would like the answers to. Also suggest that they may find other questions and answers during their research.

Business know-how

Ask students to take a minute to write down two dreams that they have, e.g. travel the world, become a famous entrepreneur, have five children, etc. Round it up at class level.

1 Look at the quotes in the top margin with the students. Ask them to match them with the questions in *Business know-how*. Then ask students to answer the questions about themselves.

2 In pairs, students compare their answers. Encourage them to explain in more detail to their partner and ask each other probing questions.

Company profile

QXL

1 In pairs, get students to discuss the questions.

2 Ask students to read *Company profile* and answer the questions.

⊙━ 2 D 3 H 4 G 5 F 6 A 7 E 8 B

Project

In pairs, students go online and research eBay – they could start by searching for 'eBay history', for example. They should make notes. Write on the board the following headings to help guide the research.

- What is eBay?
- When was it started?
- Who started it?
- Why was it started?
- What was the first item sold on eBay?
- How many people use it?
- What can you buy and sell on eBay?
- What are some strange things sold on eBay?
- How does eBay make payments safe?
- Who can use eBay?

Writing

Tell students that they are going to a sales conference in London. Read through the instructions with them and ask them to complete the email about the trip. Encourage them to use the Present Continuous.

Checklist

Go through the checklist with the students. Get them to tell you which activities in the unit helped them practise each point. Ask students if they need more practice in any of the areas.

Key words

Go through the list of words to check students' understanding.

6 Cultural awareness

Background

The development of communications technology, from the Internet to mobile phones, has brought different parts of the world closer together. Communication is now instantaneous. Decisions taken in one country can have an immediate impact in another. This increased interconnectedness is reflected in the economic and cultural spheres.

Globalization is 'the process by which businesses and organizations grow and start to operate in countries all over the world, which has been made easier by new technology and political developments' (*Oxford Business English Dictionary*). It makes previously isolated cultures and economies interdependent and interlinked.

In the economic sphere, the impact of globalization can be seen in the power and influence of multinational corporations such as Shell, Microsoft, Nestlé, and General Motors. There are over 60,000 multinational corporations throughout the world with more than half a million foreign subsidiaries. It is estimated that these corporations account for 20% of world production and 70% of world trade. Opinion is divided on whether globalization is having a positive or negative effect on local economies and cultures. However, there is no doubt that in the world of work, there is more communication and interdependence between people of different cultures and languages than ever before.

This greater contact carries both benefits and potential problems. Cultural differences may be seen in very obvious ways such as office hours, dress codes, and food. Attitudes towards punctuality, for example, may vary from one country to another, and there may be different attitudes to the use of titles in conversation and the exchange of business cards. Body language and gestures are also a rich area for making cultural faux pas. It may be important in certain cultures how you offer and accept a gift, or whether or not you can show the soles of your shoes.

There are also more subtle, and therefore potentially more 'dangerous', differences that can affect work and relationships in the workplace. Employees in different countries may have quite different attitudes towards the significance of planning, of how to manage meetings and negotiations, and the importance of teamwork. Misunderstandings may well be embarrassing, but they may also determine whether a meeting or project is a success or a failure.

So it comes as no surprise that there are many books and courses available which aim to help people work more effectively with colleagues and clients from other countries.

* Tip

A lot of cultural differences relate to body language, so it's useful to revise parts of the body and physical actions.
to shake hands, to kiss, to make eye contact, to touch, to hug, to cross your arms, to point, to bow, to pat somebody on the head

Start up

1 Before doing the quiz ask students these questions:

When you don't know someone how do you greet them in your country? Do people shake hands? Do they kiss? Do you greet adults differently from children? Do you have a special way of addressing people you don't know very well? What do you consider bad manners in your country? What sort of present do you take if you are invited for dinner at someone's house?

Then, in pairs, get students to complete the quiz with *must* or *mustn't*.

Oⲧ	1 mustn't	2 must, mustn't	3 must	4 must	5 must
	6 mustn't	7 mustn't	8 must	9 mustn't	10 mustn't

2 In pairs, get students to compare the answers to their own country. Go through this with the class. If there are students from different countries in the class, use this opportunity to discuss cultural differences. Ask students why having cultural knowledge is important in business.

➕ Additional activity

(weaker students)

If students have problems understanding the detail of the recording, go to p.124. Play the recording again and get them to follow it.

➕ Additional activity

(stronger students)

🎧 Play the recording again and ask students to focus on these questions.

1 Why was patting the child on his head a problem? Why can't she touch the son's head now?

2 Why was sitting in the back of the taxi a problem?

3 What did he do with the chopsticks that was a problem?

➕ Grammar test

Go to p.78 Teacher's Resource Book.

✴ Tip

Pronunciation of *must / mustn't*

We never pronounce the first 't' in *mustn't*. We don't usually pronounce the 't' in *must* before words beginning with consonants: *I must make that phone call.*

We pronounce the 't' in *must* before words beginning with vowels: *I must answer that letter.*

Listening

1 🎧 Look at the pictures and discuss them with the whole class.

Pre-teach: **rude**, **to pat somebody on the head**, **to look embarrassed**, **tips**, **to be offended**, **the back / front seat of a car**, **chopsticks**, **bowl**

Ask students what countries they think the situations are in. When they listen, ask them to confirm where the situations take place.

Play the recording, then discuss with the students which picture goes with which story. Ask them to tell you why.

> 🔑 A 3   B 1   C 2

2 In pairs, get students to discuss the questions. Round up and continue this discussion with the whole class.

Language spot
Talking about obligation

Look at the use of *must / mustn't* in *Start up* to talk about rules. Read the example sentences with the students. Then ask them to read the rules and decide where to put the sentences.

Go through the Grammar reference with students or set it as homework.

> 🔑 **Possible answers**
> 1   You must show your passport at the gate.
> 2   I must send that email tomorrow.
> 3   I have to do a lot of research in my job.
> 4   You mustn't smoke in this meeting room.
> 5   You don't have to come to the meeting.

1 Ask students to complete the sentences in class or for homework.

> 🔑 1 must buy   2 mustn't open   3 must call   4 doesn't have to finish
> 5 don't have to go   6 must be   7 mustn't miss   8 don't have to wear

2 Get students to talk about the rules in their workplace or school.

Pronunciation
must / mustn't

1 Get students to write *must* or *mustn't*.

> 🔑 1 must   2 mustn't   3 must   4 mustn't

2 🎧 Play the recording and get students to repeat the sentences. Ask them to tell you what they notice about the pronunciation of *must* and *mustn't*. Play the recording again and ask them to listen carefully to the 't'.

3 Listen to student's pronunciation as they describe qualities.

➕ Additional activity
(stronger students)
Have a discussion about the following question:
How does knowing about another culture help in business?

✱ Tip

Top margin
Ask students to read the quote. Ask them: *Have you had any experiences of cultural difficulties abroad?* Tell them a story from your life of cultural differences you have noticed in an English-speaking country.

➕ Additional activity

Get students to write guidelines for foreigners doing business with people in their country. Get them to brainstorm these categories:

- Greeting
- Touching
- Eye contact
- Punctuality
- Meals
- Giving gifts
- Taboos

(stronger students)
Get them to write about all the areas.
(weaker students)
Ask them to choose one or two areas to write about.

✱ Tip

Get students to choose useful verb + noun expressions from *It's my job* and translate them in their vocabulary notebook, e.g.
> *keep the appointment diary*
> *answer the phone*
> *organize meetings*
> *deal with enquiries*

✱ Tip

Call centres
Call centres are a growing business area. Many British call centres are now in India, which is English-speaking, saving up to 40% of costs. An Indian call centre worker earns less than a quarter of average earnings in Europe. A report by the BBC said that some customers were rude to Indian call centre workers because they felt the jobs should be in the UK, not India.
Read the text out to the students. Then discuss the pros and cons of locating business where wages and costs are cheaper.

Reading

1 Go through the adjectives with students. Ask them to choose adjectives that other nationalities would use about theirs. Round up at class level.

2 In pairs, get students to talk about how close people stand, how they greet, and what they talk about with strangers. Then ask students what they know about these factors concerning the behaviour of Americans.

Get students to guess if the sentences are true or false, then read the article and check.

> 🔑 1 F 2 T 3 T 4 F 5 T

3 Read the definition of stereotype in the top margin, then ask them to think of stereotypes about their culture.

Project

Ask students to choose a country or region of the world where they work or would like to work. Get students to research on the Internet how to behave in a business environment. Useful sites are: www.culturalsavvy.com. and www.executiveplanet.com.

It's my job

1 Ask students to discuss the question in pairs. Round up at class level and write a list on the board.

2 Ask students to read *It's my job* and answer the questions. Ask them if they would like to do Dermot's job. Discuss this question: *Should secretaries only be women?*

> 🔑 1 in charge of the running of the office, responsible for boss's appointments, answering the phone, dealing with enquiries
> 2 morning – open, sort, and distribute mail; day – type letters, answer the phone, send and receive emails and faxes, do administrative work, do filing and keep records; end of day – prepare outgoing mail
> 3 He meets them at reception, tells them about the company, and looks after them.

Call centre
Choosing an option

1 🎧 Ask students: *Have you ever phoned a company and heard a recorded message? What did it say?* Ask them to read the recorded message in pairs, and try to guess what goes in the gaps. Play the recording and get students to complete the gaps.

> 🔑 1 select 2 calling 3 number 4 one 5 general 6 other 7 hold

2 🎧 Get students to read the situations first then listen and tick the correct option for each person.

> 🔑 1 three 2 two 3 three

3 Get students to discuss the questions in pairs. Round up at class level. Go through the expressions with students.

Reading

1 Ask students to discuss in groups what products use famous celebrities or cartoon characters in their country. Round up at class level.

2 Get students to read the article and answer the questions.

O━ 1 McDonald's adopted a French mascot, Asterix, and serves French style coffee.
2 They do not serve beef or pork; they serve a vegetarian burger.
3 Coca-Cola makes local versions of the drink.
4 Yahoo uses local teams to analyse its international sites.
5 Revlon used Cindy Crawford instead of a local star.
6 Charities can create local solutions and fight poverty around the world.

3 Ask students to complete the summary of the article in class or for homework.

O━ 1 advantages 2 improve 3 sensitive 4 create 5 market 6 communication 7 increase

Business know-how

1 In pairs, get students to discuss the questions.

2 Ask students to read *Business know-how* and think of other tips to add to the lists. Round up at class level.

O━ **Possible answers**
shake hands, make eye contact, ask appropriate questions, use the person's name, etc.

Writing

1 Discuss the questions with the class and make notes on the board. Ask students to read the job description and compare it with their ideas.

2 Ask students to write a job description for their ideal job in class or for homework.

Checklist

Go through the checklist with the students. Get them to tell you which activities in the unit helped them practise each point. Ask the class if they need more practice in any of the areas.

Key words

Go through the list of words to check students' understanding.

➕ Additional activity

(all levels)
After exercise 1, ask students to find words or expressions in the article that mean:
1 try to do something (Para A) *seek to*
2 something that people attack (Para B) *target*
3 throw away something because you don't want it (Para B) *get rid of*
4 an animal or a toy that represents a company (Para B) *mascot*
5 a competitor (Para D) *rival*
6 give something to people (Para E) *hand out*

✳ Tip

Top margin
After doing Reading exercises 1–3, ask students to read the quote. Then ask students to discuss the question: *Is globalization good or bad?* in groups.

➕ Additional activity

(stronger students)
Ask students to write a 150–200 word article entitled: *Globalization and Glocalization*. Ask them to use their own explanations and examples. Their article should have five paragraphs: Introduction to globalization, with pros and cons; Examples of globalization; Introduction to glocalization with pros and cons; Examples of glocalization; Conclusion with personal opinion.

➕ Photocopiable activity
Getting it right
Go to p.79 Teacher's Resource Book.

7 Trade fairs

Background

Trade fairs (also called **trade shows** or **exhibitions**) are events at which many different companies producing related products showcase their new goods or services. They are popular events for both participating companies and attendees. There are over 2,500 trade fairs held annually in the USA alone. This isn't as many as in Germany, which has a long history of hosting trade fairs dating back some 800 years. Today it hosts about two thirds of the world's leading international trade fairs including the CeBIT computers fair in Hanover, which almost half a million people visited in 2005. In Europe as a whole, the 1,000 trade fairs held every year attract about 40 million visitors.

Taking part in a trade fair can be an expensive investment, with participating companies having to pay to rent exhibition space, and for the design and construction of their stand, travel, accommodation, promotional literature and 'freebies' – free items given away to attendees. However, attending a trade fair offers clear benefits to both participating companies and visitors. They are a way to make face-to-face contact, to identify suppliers, to see what the competition is doing, and to make deals, sales, and purchases. And just as companies have to prepare to make the most of the trade fair, so the visitors should be prepared, too, and have clear objectives for what they want to achieve.

Even when the trade fair is over, some of the most important work still remains to be done – the making of phone calls and the writing of emails and letters to follow-up leads, contacts, and enquiries.

Another important event in business is the **careers fair** (or **jobs fair**). These events are used by businesses to promote their companies and employment possibilities. They also offer students the opportunity to talk directly with employers, get more information about careers they are interested in, and present themselves as prospective employees. Therefore it is vital for students to go prepared with up-to-date resumes and the questions they want to have answered.

✳ Tip

freebie
an article or service given away free as a promotion. Common freebies are pens and pencils, mouse mats, bags, etc. Other names are: *business gifts, promotional items, marketing merchandise*

✳ Tip

Saying prices in English
£3.50 three (pounds) fifty
£4.05 four pounds and five pence/p
£0.87 eighty-seven pence/p
€3.50 three (euros) fifty
€4.05 four euros and five cents
€0.87 eighty-seven cents

✚ Additional activity

(weaker students)
🎧 Write these adjectives on the board and ask students to copy them. Play the recording again and get them to tick the ones they hear.
practical stupid original cheap expensive boring fun useful brilliant

Start up

Pre-teach **freebie**. Ask students to look at the pictures and discuss the questions in pairs. Round up at class level.

Listening

1 🎧 Explain that Liam and Kim are deciding which freebies their company Liberation should offer at a trade fair. Get students to listen and tick the items they choose and cross the ones they reject.

> 🔑 biro ✗   mouse mat ✗   conference folder ✗   pocket radio ✗
> conference bag ✓   stress ball ✓

2 🎧 Ask students to copy the table from the book in their notebook. Play the recording again and ask them to make notes in their table.

🔑 Item	+	−
stress balls	*good price, fun, relaxing*	
pocket radio	*nice gadget*	*wouldn't be used*
mouse mat		*people already have them*
biro		*people would lose them*
conference bag	*carries the logo, practical*	*not original*

✳ Tip

Get students to make a notebook vocabulary page for trade fairs. Ask them to translate each word.

exhibition exhibitors visitors
manufacturers buyers stand
promotional materials stand furniture
display samples leaflets catalogues
contact event organizers

Reading

1 Discuss the questions with the students. Then ask them to read the article and answer the questions.

> **O⊸** 1 To make face-to-face contact, demonstrate and launch products, test new markets, find out what customers want, find out about new developments, check out the competition, get new ideas
> 2 So that you go to the right trade fair, get a good stand position, have promotional materials and stand furniture ready, can book accommodation and transport
> 3 Ask questions, show samples, give demonstrations, take records of visitors, give out leaflets and business cards
> 4 Have a meeting to discuss how it went, follow up contacts with phone calls, letters or emails

2 Get students to write sentences about what staff should do at a trade fair in class or at home. Discuss with students the reasons for this advice. Ask them to think of other things you *should / shouldn't do* at a trade fair.

> **O⊸** You should look at a trade fair's statistics.
> You should book well in advance.
> You should order promotional materials and stand furniture.
> You should book accommodation and transport.
> Staff should be well prepared and they should ask appropriate questions.
> They should give out leaflets and business cards.
> You shouldn't neglect the contacts you made.

➕ Grammar test

Go to p.80 Teacher's Resource Book.

✳ Tip

Top margin

● Before turning to p.42, ask students to write a definition of **trade fair**. Then read the definition with them on p.42. Do they think their definition included all the points?

● Get students to close their books and dictate what Bengt Svensson says. Then ask them to open their books on p.42 and check.

Language spot

should / shouldn't

Get students to read and complete the rules (1 = weaker, 2 = advice). Emphasize that *should / shouldn't* isn't as strong as *must / mustn't*, and so is used frequently to give opinions and advice.

Go through the Grammar reference with students or set it as homework.

1 Ask students to complete the tips in class or as homework.

> **O⊸** You **should** get there early to set up the stand
> You **should** wear your badge at all times
> You **shouldn't** leave your bags and coats around
> You **should** wear smart clothes and be well-presented
> You **should** be well-informed about your company
> You **shouldn't** eat or drink on the stand
> You **should** carry a notebook with you
> You **should** have plenty of promotional materials
> You **shouldn't** gossip with your colleagues
> You **should** get interested visitors to leave their details

➕ Additional activity

(all levels)

After *Language spot* exercise 2, ask the groups to report their advice to the class. The class should then vote for the best solution.

2 Read through the problem with students. Ask them to individually make a note of their advice.

3 In groups, get students to discuss the problem and write their advice.

➕ **Writing bank**
Letters 2 – Enquiries
Go to p.56 Student's Book.

Speaking

Students A and B read their problems, then take it in turns to tell each other about their problems and give each other advice. The student giving advice should think of different solutions. The student with the problem should agree or disagree with the suggestions and explain why.

> **⚲ Ideas for advice**
> **Student A** Problem 1: show the boss what you have achieved; ask the boss why you don't get promoted; look for another job; Problem 2: take sleeping pills; read books about relaxation; prepare well; learn to meditate; rehearse the talk with a colleague; change to a job where you don't have to do presentations
> **Student B** Problem 1: change job; ask to talk to your boss and discuss it; change department; talk to Human Resources; Problem 2: plan your work better; do a bit every day; work an extra hour every day; go on a course on time management

✱ Tip

miso is added to soups, sauces, and dishes. It is usually made of fermented soya beans.
teriyaki ingredients are roasted or grilled and then put in a dark shiny sauce.
takoyaki fried round balls made of octopus and other ingredients
sashimi very fresh raw seafood, thinly sliced, served with a dipping sauce
tataki Small slices of meat or fish are stuffed and rolled. They are fried quickly and served with a ginger sauce.

9 to 5

Eating out

1 In pairs, get students to discuss the questions. Ask students if they have ever eaten Japanese food.

2 Get students to guess what is being said in each picture.

3 🎧 Get students to listen again and decide if the sentences are true or false.

> **⚲** 1 T   2 T   3 F   4 F   5 F   6 T

4 🎧 Look at the menu and explain the ingredients (see *Tip*). Get students to guess what is being said, then listen and make notes of what Lisa and Richard order. Ask if their guesses were correct.

> **⚲** Lisa orders chicken noodle soup and beef teriyaki; Richard orders miso soup and takoyaki. They also order a bottle of fizzy water.

5 🎧 Get students to listen again and tick the expressions they hear.

> **⚲** Are you ready to order?   I'd like …   I'll have …   Can you tell me what … is?
> I don't like the sound of that.   What's the soup like?   It's delicious!

➕ **Additional activity**

(weaker students)
You can simplify the role-play by explaining the items on the menu to the whole class in their own language if necessary. Then get students to role-play ordering the food but not asking about the menu.

Speaking

Go through the *Expressions* list with the students. Ask them to repeat the sentences after you, paying attention to pronunciation and intonation.

Divide the class into groups of three, with one stronger student in each group as waiter. The other two students are customers. The 'customers' will have to ask for more information about the dishes.

Get the 'waiters' together and help them with the menu explanations.

After a short time, interrupt and ask a strong group to perform the role-play, helping them where necessary. Then ask all the groups to try the task again, swapping roles if they like.

* Tip

Food and cooking methods
Start these lists on the board and ask students to work in groups and add to them.
Meat: lamb, beef, chicken, pork, bacon, minced meat
Fish: salmon, cod, tuna, prawns, shellfish
Vegetables: potatoes, peas, pepper, aubergine, onion, lettuce, cabbage
Fruit: apple, orange, pear, banana, strawberry
Other basics: rice, pastry / pie, bread, cheese, eggs, milk
Cooking methods: fry, grill, boil, bake, steam

✚ Additional activity

(all levels)
Ask students what they think are the qualities that make a successful business.

✚ Additional activity

(stronger students)
Ask students to present their report in an oral presentation to the class. Encourage the class to ask questions.

✚ Photocopiable activity
Careers fair
Go to p.81 Teacher's Resource Book.

✚ Writing bank
Letters 3 – Following up
Go to p.57 Student's Book.

Company profile
Yo!

1 Get students to answer the questions and discuss their answers.

> ○━ 1 an entrepreneur   2 to open conveyor-belt sushi restaurants in the UK   3 In 1997   4 a positive attitude, enthusiasm, realism, and the ability to handle failure   5 *Yotel! Yo! Japan*   6 Students' own answers

2 Ask students to find the words and translate them in class or for homework.

Project

1 Get students to research the entrepreneurs on the Internet. Ask them to organize their ideas under the following headings:

- Who is he / she? where born, education, etc.
- What was his / her big idea?
- When / How did he / she start in business?
- What does he / she believe makes a successful business?
- What are his / her companies now?
- What are his / her future ideas?
- What do you find interesting / surprising / inspirational?

2 Ask students to write their report with questions and answers.

Business know-how

1 Ask students to read about careers fairs and discuss what sort of companies they would like to meet there.

2 Ask students to read the tips and choose the three most important, giving their reasons.

Writing

1 Ask students to read the email and answer the question (answer = c).

2 Go through the situation with the students. Then get them to write the email in class or for homework.

Checklist

Go through the checklist with the students. Get them to tell you which activities in the unit helped them practise each point. Ask the class if they need to do any more practice in any of the areas.

Key words

Go through the list of words to check students' understanding.

8 Advertising

Background

In the UK alone, companies spend over £14 billion on advertising every year. Obviously, businesses think that advertising works – but what do they hope it will achieve? A core aim is to increase sales by making the Unique Selling Point (or USP) of the product or service clear to potential customers, whether this is a lower price, superior quality, or special features. It also aims to:

- attract new customers by stimulating interest
- change people's views or attitudes
- differentiate the product or service from competitors'
- encourage brand-switching from rival products
- make a brand or business better known to the public.

When the decision to advertise has been taken, companies then have to choose which media to use, from television to the Internet. The choice will depend on the market segment the company wants to reach (age group, business or domestic, male or female, etc.); the geographical spread of potential customers (local, national, or international); and above all, the budget the company has to spend.

The various media used for advertising carry advantages and disadvantages. Television can reach enormous audiences, and the advertisement can be repeated any number of times. It is, however, extremely expensive, so would only be suitable for mass-consumption products. Advertising with billboards is much cheaper, but the advertisements must be placed in strategic locations and the message they contain has to be concise. Commercial radio is again a more economical option, and is particularly effective when targeting a local market.

Once the medium has been chosen, advertisers employ a range of techniques to get their message across. They may repeat key information to ensure that we remember it, make an emotional appeal to us (for example, the maternal appeal of babies), or employ the scientific endorsement of experts or the celebrity appeal of film stars or models.

So what are the main rules of advertising? They are neatly expressed in the acronym AIDA:

- **Attract** the attention of potential customers
- gain **Interest** in the product
- create a **Desire** for its benefits
- tell customers how to take **Action**

If the advertisement achieves all four aims, then it should be a success.

Start up

1 Ask students to discuss the questions in groups.

2 Ask them to look at the extracts from ads and match them to the products.

> 🔑 a holiday destination = A   washing powder = D   fridge = H
> furniture = C   pet food = B   ferries = E   beds = G   bathrooms = F

➕ **Additional activity**
(all levels)
Take in English language newspapers and magazines. In pairs, get students to go through looking for adjectives in the advertisements.

➕ **Additional activity**
(weaker students)
Write these adjectives on the board: *tasty, bright, new, effective, brilliant, strongest, best, cheapest*
Ask students to tell you what products might be advertised using them.

3 Ask students to find the adjectives either as they are in the box or in the superlative forms. They copy and complete the table.

🔑 Adjective	Describing
crunchy / crunchier	pet food
free	design
bright / brightest	whites
cool / coolest	look
tasty / tastier	pet food
close / closer	destination
international	authority
popular	holiday destination
easy / easier	access

➕ Grammar test

Go to p.82 Teacher's Resource Book.

Language spot
Comparatives and superlatives

Ask students to complete the rules. Go through the Grammar reference with students or set it as homework.

> **O—** 1 comparatives   2 superlatives   3 *one of the most / least*
> 4 *more*   5 *most*

1 Ask students to complete the article.

> **O—** 2 the most expensive   3 cheaper   4 smaller   5 more people
> 6 the easiest ways   7 less   8 larger   9 lower prices
> 10 the most suitable   11 better than

2 In groups, ask students to discuss products they know.

3 In pairs, students choose one of the products and write an advertisement.

Reading

1 Discuss what sort of products different types of people (e.g. families, business people, beautiful women, etc.) usually advertise.

> **O—** **Possible answers**
> young men: beer, mobile phones, cars, snacks, razors, clothes, holidays
> young women: beauty products, perfume, clothes, drinks, cars, holidays
> children: sweets, food, toys
> housewives: food, beauty products, cleaning products, air fresheners
> business people: computers, airlines, cars, mobile phones, hotels
> teenagers: computers, drinks, snacks, beauty products
> families: food, drinks, holidays, baby food and products, cars
> secretaries: dieting products, soft drinks, office equipment
> old people: insurance, vitamins, holidays

2 Ask students to read the text and match the headings to paragraphs.

> **O—** Scientific authority = D   Negative feelings = C   Association of ideas = F
> Repetition = A   Hype = B

3 Get students to read the article again and answer the questions.

> **O—** 1 B   2 E   3 F   4 D

Listening

🎧 Ask students to listen and note down types of product and techniques.

> **O—** 1 flowers ordered online and delivered – plays on feelings of guilt, and has emotional appeal
> 2 holidays – uses the association of ideas

➕ Additional activity

(all levels)

Take in English language newspapers and magazines. In pairs, ask students to find the advert that they like best and explain why they like it. Then ask them to find adverts that provide examples of each technique: Scientific authority, Negative feelings, Repetition, Hype, Emotional appeal, Association of ideas.

✳ Tip
Top margin

● Read out the first two quotes. Ask students to paraphrase each one, and put the opposite argument.
The best ad is a good product.
paraphrase: Advertising can help sell a product, but in the end it has to be a good product; **opposite argument**: Even a good product can't be sold without advertising.
Word of mouth is the best medium of all.
paraphrase: If a product works, people will tell each other about it; **opposite argument**: Word of mouth will never be enough to sell a lot of a product.
● Read out the last quote. Ask students to tell you what they think B. Earl Puckett advertises (cosmetics). Do they agree that most adverts for cosmetics and clothes are designed to make women unhappy?

✚ Additional activity

(all levels)

Ask students to read the article again and find words and expressions that mean:

1 a short phrase used in advertisements *slogan*
2 a description that makes something seem better, worse, etc. than it is *exaggeration*
3 not precise *vague*
4 to control somebody without them realizing *manipulate*
5 a statement showing you support something *endorsement*
6 attractive and exciting *glamorous*
7 qualities of a man *manliness*
8 fashionably simple *minimalist*

✱ Tip

oversee to make sure that other workers do their work
liaise to work closely with someone and exchange information
brief to give someone information about something so they can deal with it
negotiate to try to reach agreement by formal discussion
supervise to be in charge of something and to make sure everything is done correctly
deliver to do or produce what you promised

✚ Photocopiable activity
Promoting products
Go to p.83 Teacher's Resource Book.

Reading

1 Ask students to look at the picture and speculate about the company.

2 Get students to read the article and decide if the sentences are true or false.

> ⊙━ 2 T   3 F   4 T   5 F   6 F

Project

Governments often advertise and promote areas such as nursing, the army, and teaching through adverts. Get students to work in groups and allocate roles. Agree with the class whether they are going to write an advert or a summary. Suggest they look at unit 4 for ideas. Have a vote on the best advert.

Call centre
Checking information

1 🎧 Go through the notes with the students. Then play the recording and get them to correct them.

> ⊙━ Stephen George 020 78879986   Afternoon more convenient

2 🎧 Go through the *Expressions* with the students. Then play the recording again and get students to tick them.

> ⊙━ Sorry, what did you say?   Did you say …?   Sorry, I didn't catch that.
> Would you mind saying that again?

Pronunciation
Emphasizing information

Play the recording from *Call centre* again. Stop after each exchange and ask students to tell you which words the speaker stresses in order to correct the information (*Stephen, seven* and *six, afternoon*).

🎧 Go through the sentences and get students to speculate about how they will sound. Then play the recording and get them to underline the stressed words and numbers.

> ⊙━ 1 No, I said the <u>Toyota</u> was more expensive.   2 No, I said 07903.
> 3 No, it's <u>less</u> compatible.   4 No, it's 37, <u>Wessex</u> Street.

Speaking

Go through the *Expressions* list with the students. Ask them to repeat the sentences after you.

Explain that each student has information written down. One person has to give information to the other. They need to clarify that the information they have is correct. Write on the board:

Student A has written: Power Hotel   Student B wants to book: Tower Hotel
Student A: *Did you say Power Hotel?*   Student B: *No, I said <u>Tower</u> Hotel.*

Get students to do the activity. Ask some pairs to come out in front of the class and perform the dialogues.

It's my job

1 Ask students to read the article and answer the questions.

> **O┳** 1 Just over two years
> 2 She writes the words in adverts, brainstorms ideas in a small team, works with the Art Director
> 3 Be creative, be able to accept criticism, get on well with people, work under pressure

2 Get students to discuss the questions in pairs.

Business know-how

Discuss with students how businesses use creativity (new ideas, improvements, better sales, better products, new solutions). Ask them if they do anything creative in their free time.

Ask students to go through the tips in pairs.

Writing

1 Ask students if they have ever bought or sold something online. Ask them what they need to know if they are buying used clothes online (size, condition, colour, make, reason for selling).

Ask students to read the advert and answer the questions.

> **O┳** 1 leather jacket
> 2 fashionable, good condition, brown, metal buttons, three pockets
> 3 too small

2 Ask students to do this exercise in class or for homework. Provide them with the help they may need to describe the individual items.

Checklist

Go through the checklist with the students. Get them to tell you which activities in the unit helped them practise each point. Ask the class if they need more practice in any of the areas.

Key words

Go through the list of words to check students' understanding.

➕ Additional activity

(stronger students)

Ask them to write a reasons for each of the *Business know-how* tips, e.g.:

- If you have quiet time to think you give your mind an opportunity to create.
- If you think your ideas are stupid, you stop yourself being creative.
- If you look around you, you get new ideas.
- If you learn new skills, your mind becomes more flexible.
- If you have a strange idea, someone else may be able to develop it.
- If you have fun, you allow your brain to make new connections.

➕ Writing bank
Faxes – Giving directions
Go to p.60 Student's Book.

9 Fashion and style

Background

You might be the type who reads fashion magazines, checks out what celebrities are wearing, and buys the latest styles. You might generally wear 'business' clothes and simply try to look smart. Or you might prefer casual clothes and have no interest in fashion and trends whatsoever. Whatever the case, fashion is something that we deal with everyday, from choosing what to wear in the morning, to buying clothes in designer stores or high-street chains. And fashion is also a vast international business, employing millions of people in a range of jobs from designers, stylists, and company directors to buyers, sellers, and manufacturers.

From the glamorous world of exclusive boutiques to budget stores, fashion means big business. In the world of high fashion, LVMH owns Louis Vuitton, Hermès, Kenzo, Fendi, and Pucci among others, and has annual sales of over $11.5 billion. Pinault-Printemps-Redoute SA, which owns Gucci, Yves St Laurent, Sergio Rossi, etc. has annual sales of nearly $25 billion. Meanwhile in 2004, Gap generated $16.3 billion of sales worldwide through their 3,000 stores. Another recent success story is Zara, the Spanish fashion brand founded in La Coruña in 1975. There are now over 400 Zara stores worldwide. With annual sales increasing by around 25% in the last five years, it is one of the world's fastest-growing retailers. One factor in its success is its incredible turnover of new products. In a typical year it will introduce about 11,000 new garments, and many of these will be in the shops for only a few weeks. For a high-street store, it means that the clothes it sells are also rather 'exclusive'.

'The apparel oft proclaims the man', wrote Shakespeare in *Hamlet*. Or in other words, what we wear and how we choose to present ourselves, says something about who we are. In a recent study conducted by the University of Strathclyde, over 90% of UK bosses considered that the right attitude and appearance, including dress sense, were more important than skills and experience. Hardly surprisingly, many books and websites offer advice on how we should present ourselves at interviews and in the workplace generally. The clear message is: if you want to succeed, take care of your appearance. Don't wear weekend clothes to the workplace. Look businesslike but stylish. And if you *look* professional, then people will assume that you *are* professional.

✳ Tip

Revise clothes and accessories vocabulary with students, for example:
shirt tie trousers jacket suit jeans sweatshirt sweater skirt dress top shoes boots trainers belt scarf tracksuit coat leggings hat cap T-shirt

Start up

Get students to work in pairs and do the quiz. When they have finished they score one point for each 'yes' answer. Ask them to read their score.

Listening 1

1 🎧 Tell students they are going to hear two friends doing the questionnaire.

Play the recording and ask students to make notes of Alex's answers (yes or no) for each question. Then play the recording again and do the same for Maria.

Oₜ **Alex**	1 no, yes	2 no	3 yes	4 no	5 yes	6 yes	7 no	8 yes	9 no	10 no
Maria	1 yes	2 yes	3 no	4 yes	5 yes	6 yes	7 no	8 yes	9 yes	10 yes

2 Get students to calculate the scores for Alex and Maria. Then discuss their scores with the whole class.

Oₜ Alex's score: 5   Maria's score: 8

✳ Tip

Adjectives

Ask students to choose from these adjectives. They can write them in their vocabulary notebook and translate them.
simple elegant sporty fashionable healthy eco-friendly comfortable authentic uncomfortable stylish old-fashioned unusual basic fun

➕ Additional activity

(weaker students)

Ask students to underline sentences using *although, when, while* in the text. Discuss their use.

✳ Tip

Top margin

Read the quotes with the students and discuss them.
Quote 1 introduces the idea that fashion helps people create an identity for themselves and identify with a group.
Quote 2 introduces the idea that fashion inevitably becomes out of date – something which is encouraged by the fashion industry.

Reading

1 Get students to look at the pictures and describe the shoes.

2 Ask students to read the article and answer the questions.

> 🔑 1 It doesn't promote a luxury lifestyle; it believes in simplicity and authenticity.
> 2 In Majorca, Spain
> 3 A traditional recycled Majorcan shoe
> 4 A culture brand
> 5 Online shopping and hotels
> 6 Nike are making cheaper, recyclable shoes.

Vocabulary

Get students to match the nouns.

> 🔑 1 e 2 c 3 a 4 b 5 d

Project

1 Get students to do the project in groups. Give them a time limit of half an hour. Go round and encourage students to make decisions and complete the task within the time limit.

2 Ask the groups to choose one student to present the project. Encourage the class to ask questions. Get the students to vote for the best product.

Listening 2

1 Get students to match the jobs and descriptions.

> 🔑 1 d 2 c 3 b 4 a

2 🎧 Before listening, ask students to read through the article and try to guess what words go in the gaps. Then play the recording and get students to complete the gaps. Stop and start the recording after each paragraph and ask students to discuss their answers with their partner before continuing.

> 🔑 1 2003 2 Italy 3 Germany 4 two years 5 fashion shows
> 6 New York 7 three months 8 ten years 9 2004
> 10 Communication

3 🎧 Get students to cover the article and to listen again and write the names.

4 Get students to check their answers by uncovering the article.

> 🔑 1 Antonia 2 Lisa 3 John 4 Mark 5 Lisa 6 John 7 Mark 8 Antonia

✚ Grammar test
Go to p.84 Teacher's Resource Book.

Language spot
Present Perfect

Ask students to read the rules and put the examples with the correct rule.

> 🔑 1 I've gained some good experience.
> 2 I've worked as a fashion buyer for the last two years.
> 3 I haven't been involved in design work yet.
> 4 Have you designed for women yet?

Go through the Grammar reference with students or set it for homework.

1 Get students to discuss their last six months, using the Present Perfect.

2 🎧 Play the recording and get students to tick what Antonia has done.

> 🔑 quality control ✓   management ✗   sales ✓   telephones ✗
> current orders ✓   design ✗

3 Get students to complete the sentences in class or for homework.

> 🔑 1 since 2 for (number) 3 for (number) 4 since 5 for (number) 6 since

9 to 5
Making requests

1 Ask students to look at the picture and answer the question.

2 🎧 Play the recording and get students to write the initials.

> 🔑 1 R 2 R 3 J 4 S 5 R

3 🎧 Get students to try to complete the gaps from memory. Then play the recording and get them to complete the gaps. Discuss at class level why the questions are formulated in different ways. (1 These are close to being polite imperatives as Richard is the boss. 2 This is politer, because Joe is asking a favour. 3 This again is a polite request.)

> 🔑 1 can you, can you   2 Would you, printing   3 Could you possibly

4 Discuss the question with the whole class.

> 🔑 Expression 2

✚ Additional activity
(weaker students)
Before doing the *Speaking* activity get students to make polite requests in the classroom in pairs, e.g. *lend me your dictionary / open the window / lend me a pen / help me with my homework / get me a glass of water / etc.*

Speaking

Go through the *Expressions* list with the whole class. Ask them to repeat the sentences after you, paying attention to pronunciation and intonation. You can use the recording to do this activity if you prefer.

Divide students into pairs and ask them to study their *Speaking activities*. Get them to do the activity. Interrupt the activity halfway through and give students feedback on their performance before asking them to continue.

✱ Tip

Top margin

● Ask students what the word Gap means. Get them to read the first piece of information and discuss the generation gap. Ask them if they think there is still a generation gap or if it was bigger in the 1960s. Do they think Gap is a good name for a clothing store?

● Ask students to read the second piece of information. What else do they know about Bono's activities (He is the lead singer with U2. He helped organize Live 8, the international rock concert which raised millions for charity in 2005.) Ask students: *Do you think initiatives like the Red Collection are a good idea?*

✱ Tip

revenue the money received by a business for goods or services
earnings the profit that a business makes
go into to start working in a particular field

➕ Photocopiable activity
Dressing for work
Go to p.85 Teacher's Resource Book.

➕ Writing bank
Emails 4 – Inviting
Go to p.58 Student's Book.

Company profile
Gap Inc.

Ask students to tell you everything they know about Gap – its image, the type of clothes it sells, whether they like the clothes, etc. Make notes on the board.

Student A is going to read the information on the page and Student B is going to read different information on p.110. Students must try hard to remember the key information, making notes if they like. When they have finished they should cover their information before doing the speaking activity. At the end of the activity ask students whether the notes on the board have been confirmed by the information or not.

Business know-how

1 Ask students to discuss the questions in pairs. Then round up at class level. Encourage students to give their opinions. Ask them to tell you who they believe is well-dressed in business or politics in their country, and who doesn't dress appropriately.

2 Ask students to read the tips in pairs and discuss which ones they agree and disagree with. With the whole class, make a list of extra points that they would suggest for doing business in their country.

Writing

1 Ask students to read the invitations. Discuss with them the different ways you would dress for each event. Then get them to read the example. Would the boys wear similar clothes? What would the girls in the class wear?

Ask students to write what they would wear for each event in class or for homework.

2 Go through the *Expressions* at class level. Then ask students to write invitations to other people in the class – make sure that each students will receive an invitation. The students then answer the invitation they receive.

Checklist

Go through the checklist with the students. Get them to tell you which activities in the unit helped them practise each point. Ask the class if they need more practice in any of the areas.

Key words

Go through the list of words to check students' understanding.

10 Technology

Background

Technological developments have had a profound effect on the way businesses operate, and the way people work within them. Email allows us to send documents across the world at the press of a key; its immediacy means that face-to-face meetings are becoming less and less frequent – and even these can take place via satellite if necessary; and the Internet compresses the basic functions of business – advertising, informing, selling, etc. – so that they can take place almost simultaneously on a single computer screen.

E-business has become essential to companies, and they have to develop an e-business strategy to fully exploit the opportunities it offers. This strategy will include:

● selling and receiving payments online
● providing customer support and information
● online marketing
● the analysis of how customers use the online facility and what they are interested in.

While computer-controlled warehouses and machinery have led to some redundancies, new technology has also created jobs such as computer technicians, web designers, and systems analysts.

Most workspaces are now furnished with computers and printers. Employees will probably have their own workspace, although in some environments a 'hot-desking' policy may be in operation. In this case, employees simply plug in their laptops in the workspace of their choice. Technology has released us from the necessity of working in one place all the time. Wi-Fi (short for Wireless Fidelity) technology provides complete autonomy over where we work – while intranet (private company network), and internet facilities mean staff can work in any location.

As we can keep in contact with colleagues and clients irrespective of location, with instant access to whatever information we need, many employees are now able to work from home (teleworking or telecommuting), or choose to go freelance.

In the near future, videoconferencing from all PCs will make many 'physical' face-to-face meetings redundant. And ultra-thin monitors, ultra-fast broadband, and ultra-powerful mobile phones will continue to have an impact on the environment in which we work, and the way we work.

✳ Tip

BlackBerry a wireless handheld device that supports email, mobile phone, text messaging, and web surfing
Wi-Fi allows people with a wireless computer to connect to the Internet
L8 late (in text messaging)
gbps a measure of data transferral - gigabits per second
ISP Internet Service Provider
back-up a copy or spare of something that you can use if the original one is lost or unavailable

Start up

Ask the students to do the quiz together in pairs. Get them to calculate their score and read their profile.

Reading

1 At class level, ask students to discuss the questions.

2 Get students to read the article and answer the questions.

1 servers and clients
2 a 'gateway' server
3 Your request is sent by your ISP to the host server. Then you can view the web page.
4 It was the first computer network, developed by the US military in the 1950s and adapted by scientists in the 1960s. Its disadvantage was that it was complex and difficult to use.
5 Tim Berners-Lee invented the World Wide Web.

➕ Additional activity

(all levels)

Get students to read the article again, find the relevant Passive sentences and complete these sentences in the Active form.

1 Servers store … (the information you seek.)
2 An ISP operates a … ('gateway' server.)
3 The US military developed … (the first computer network.)
4 Scientists adapted … (the first computer network in 1960 so they could share information.)
5 The World Wide Web revolutionized… (the Internet.)
6 Tim Berners-Lee invented … (the World Wide Web.)

➕ Grammar test

Go to p.86 Teacher's Resource Book.

✳ Tip

Top margin

Ask students to read the information. Which fact do they find most surprising?

➕ Additional activity

(all levels)

Ask students to close their books. Then ask them to recreate the tips. Give them these prompts on the board:

- privacy
- flaming
- instant reply
- forwarding
- politeness
- shortness
- tone
- quoting
- abbreviations

Language spot

The Passive

Go through the rules with students. Then go through the Grammar reference with students or set it for homework.

> ⚷ 1 is passed on   2 is connected   3 was invented

1 Get students to underline the Present Passive and circle the Past Passive in the text. Explain that articles that talk about processes and historical developments often use the Passive.

> ⚷ **Present Passive**: are involved, is stored, is located, is connected, is operated, is passed on, is passed
> **Past Passive**: was developed, was adapted, was called, was revolutionized, was invented, was introduced

2 Get students to use the sentences to write a paragraph.

> ⚷ Then the date is printed on the stamps (by another machine). The mail is then put into separate postbags (by machines). Then the bags are loaded onto lorries (by postal workers). The mail is taken to local sorting offices (by lorries). After that, the mail is sorted into individual areas (by postal workers). And finally the mail is delivered (by the postal workers).

Reading

1 Get students to discuss the questions in pairs. Then round up at class level.

2 Ask students to read the article and discuss their answers in pairs.

3 Ask students to look at the emails and decide what is wrong with each one.

> ⚷ 2 Frankie shouldn't use so many abbreviations and emoticons.
> 3 Claudia should avoid flaming.
> 4 Keiko shouldn't expect an instant answer.

Listening

1 🎧 Ask students to try and guess the missing words. Then play the recording and get them to complete the gaps.

> ⚷ 1 message   2 job   3 automatically   4 people
> 5 grammar   6 capitals   7 document   8 recipient

2 Get students to discuss the tips.

Reading

1 Tell students a story about when you had trouble with technology (e.g. an email that went to the wrong person, the day you lost an important document, the day you lost all your mobile phone contacts, etc.). Ask them to read the anecdotes and match them with the titles.

➕ Additional activity
(weaker students)
Ask students to close their books and dictate a couple of the anecdotes. This provides useful reinforcement of vocabulary and practises recognition of punctuation.

➕ Photocopiable activity
Going online
Go to p.87 Teacher's Resource Book.

➕ Additional activity
(stronger students)
Ask students to write an anecdote for homework.

> **O━** E-ticket – no ticket = Paolo   No computer, no work = Vanessa
> Oops – wrong email address! = Jake   Can you hear me? = Simone

2 Ask students to discuss in groups similar experiences they have had with technology.

Pronunciation
Email addresses

1 🎧 get students to discuss how to read the addresses. Then play the recording. Play the recording again and stop and ask students to repeat the addresses.

2 🎧 Ask students to listen for the individual elements.

> **O━** 1 at   2 dot   3 underscore   4 hyphen   5 upper case G   6 lower case g

3 🎧 Play the recording and get students to write the addresses. Play it as often as necessary.

> **O━** 1 alex_bozoukova@linknet.co.uk   2 kirkham.jed@LBF-marketing.com

Call centre
Taking a message

1 🎧 Play the recording and get students to make a note of the information.

> **O━** name of caller = Joe Enderby
> company = JYT
> reason for call = He wants to talk to Robert Adams about his recent order.

2 🎧 Go through the *Expressions* with the students. Play the recording and get them to number the expressions in the order they hear them.

> **O━** What can I do for you? 9
> (Tina Jones) speaking. 1
> Can I speak to (Robert Adams), please? 4
> I'll see that (Robert) gets the message. 7
> How can I help you? 2
> I'm afraid he's away from his desk. 5
> This is (Joe Enderby). 3
> Am I calling at a convenient time? 8
> Could you ask him to call me? 6

➕ Additional activity
(weaker students)
Get the students to write out one of the dialogues from the role-play for homework.

Speaking

1 Go through the *Expressions* list with the students. Ask them to repeat the sentences after you. You can use the recording to do this activity if you prefer.

Divide the class into pairs. Go through the *Speaking activity* instructions with the students. Do the role-play with a strong student, then get the class to do it several times.

It's my job

1 Get students to work in pairs and discuss the question.

> **O—π Possible answers**
> deals with computer problems, installs new software and hardware, launches new IT resources, trains people.

+ Additional activity
(stronger students)
Ask students to write a short summary of Gary's job in about 100 words.

2 Ask students to read about Gary and answer the first question.

> **O—π** Skills and qualities: 'people' skills, technical skills, multitasking, managing tasks, ability to understand the wider business context

Discuss the second question with the whole class.

> **O—π Possible answer**
> It is probably necessary to develop all the skills Gary mentions, except the technical ones, in all business situations.

Business know-how

1 Ask students to work in pairs and make notes of their ideas. Then round up at class level.

2 Ask students to read the tips and compare the class ideas with them.

+ Writing bank
Emails 5 – Answering queries
Go to p.61 Student's Book.

Writing

1 Ask students to read Katie's email and identify the problems.

> **O—π** She hasn't put a subject; she hasn't opened with a greeting or closed with her name; she expects the email to be read immediately; the 'tone of voice' could be more polite.

2 Get students to answer the email following the advice on p.74 and p.75.

> **O—π** From: Dan Ross   To: Adam Krasinski   CC: Katie Cavendish
> Subject: Sales figures and company organization document
>
> Dear Adam
> Katie Cavendish has asked me to send you the attached document 'Personnel'. It explains recent changes to the company organization. She has also asked you to send her your latest sales figures by tomorrow morning. I hope that you are all well in the Polish office.
> All the best
> Dan Ross

Checklist

Go through the checklist with the students. Get them to tell you which activities in the unit helped them practise each point. Ask the class if they need more practice in any of the areas.

Key words

Go through the list of words to check students' understanding.

11 Job satisfaction

Background

Why do people work? Apart from the need to earn a salary, to have a feeling of security and perhaps of self-importance, people also like to feel that they are doing something useful and they are using their skills and creativity. Job satisfaction is an important motivation in the workplace. Businesses are increasingly aware of this, and try to ensure that their staff are happy, challenged, and motivated. In the office, this may involve:

- job enlargement – employees are given more tasks to do at the same level. This guarantees greater variety of work.
- job enrichment – employees are given greater responsibility and more demanding tasks. As their job becomes more challenging, so it becomes more interesting.

Greater job satisfaction can be achieved through increased pay, performance-related bonuses, and other benefits, but **work-life balance** is important, too. If the pressures and responsibilities of work eat into employees' free time – the time they need to spend with families, friends, or simply relaxing – a stressed, discontented workforce is the result. Companies can offer various initiatives to promote this:

- **flexi-work** – employees work a fixed number of hours per day, but they can vary when they start and finish

- **a shorter working week** – employees work one less day a week with a salary reduction, or do five days' work in four
- **teleworking** – employees work from home for a part of the week, keeping in contact with the office via computer
- **job sharing** – two people share the same job and divide the salary
- **career breaks** – employees take a sabbatical, usually unpaid, from work.

Governments also legislate to ensure that workers have certain rights at work. These may cover their health and safety, equality of opportunities and pay, and statutory holidays and other leave. In the UK, employment rights include:

- no employee may be discriminated against on grounds of gender, race or sexual orientation
- employees must not be harassed or victimized
- employees cannot be forced to work more than 48 hours per week, and are be free to choose whether to work on Sundays
- they can take the legal allowance of maternity or paternity leave
- they can apply for flexible working hours (after working for a minimum of 26 weeks for a company)
- 16–17-year-olds can have time off for studying or training.

➕ Additional activity
(all levels)
Ask students to add any words and expressions from the article to their vocabulary notebook with translations.

➕ Additional activity
(all levels)
Noun phrases
Ask students to underline expressions using the *–ing* form. Explain that you can create noun phrases with these expressions. For example:
Getting on with people is important.
Having fun at work can increase productivity.
Ask students to write sentences using the phrases they underlined.
getting on with people having fun finding work challenging being treated as an individual having a social life being respected being trusted expressing your opinions and ideas using your skills and talents being informed

Start up

1 Get students to work in pairs and discuss the question.

2 Ask students to read the article individually and choose the ten factors they think are most important.

3 Ask students to work in pairs and discuss their choices.

Listening

1 🎧 Go through the exercise with students first. Check they understand the points. Then play the recording and ask students to match the names with the points.

Play the recording again and ask students to answer the question: Are they happy or unhappy?

🔑 1 c 2 d 3 e 4 a 5 b
Nuria: unhappy   Dylan: unhappy   Beate: happy   Andy: happy
Laura: unhappy

2 🎧 Play the recording again and complete the sentences.

> 🔑 1 informed   2 bosses   3 staff   4 positive   5 manager   6 paid

3 Ask students to work in groups and discuss the caller's opinions. What do they think makes a good workplace? Which one of the points that the callers made do they think is most important?

9 to 5
Making sure

1 Go through the instructions with the students. Discuss the questions with the whole class.

> 🔑 **Possible answers**
> They might feel nervous, excited, stressed. They might take: PowerPoint presentation, laptop, pendrive, disks, handouts, promotional material, artwork, DVDs, tickets, passport, mobile phone, etc.

2 🎧 Go through the list with the students. Then play the recording.

> 🔑 1 L   2 J   3 J   4 J   5 L   6 R

3 🎧 Play the recording again and get students to tick the expressions they hear.

> 🔑 Don't worry.   That's a good idea.   That's right.   No problem.
> Of course I will.

4 Discuss the questions at class level.

> 🔑 **Possible answers**
> He should meet with his team in advance and decide who does what, write a list, allocate more time to preparation

Language spot
Question tags

Go through the grammar with the students and ask them to complete the rules. Go through the Grammar reference with students or set it as homework.

> 🔑 negative, positive

1 Get students to complete the exercise in class or for homework.

> 🔑 1 did you   2 wasn't he   3 won't you   4 did you   5 can't she

➕ **Grammar test**
Go to p.88 Teacher's Resource Book.

➕ **Additional activity**
(for weaker students)
Play this game. Divide the class into two teams. Read out the beginnings of these questions. The first team to call out the correct ending gets a point.
1 You've booked the room, _____?
   (haven't you)
2 She hasn't got a laptop, _____?
   (has she)
3 They don't eat fish, _____?
   (do they)
4 Harry can type very fast, _____?
   (can't he)
5 I left my bag here, _____? (didn't I)
6 We're meeting Patrick tomorrow,
   _____? (aren't we)
7 Karl and Mohammed are in Paris,
   _____? (aren't they)
8 You didn't bring the presentation,
   _____? (did you)
9 I'm going to get the five o'clock train,
   _____? (aren't I)
10 Maria will send you the report,
   _____? (won't she)

2 Get students to write sentences with question tags.

> 2 You don't like the meeting room, do you?
> 3 I don't think the bedrooms are warm enough, are they?
> 4 Everyone else is having breakfast, aren't they?
> 5 The meal last night was terrible, wasn't it?

➕ Additional activity

(all levels)

Get students to write up a dialogue based on the *Speaking* activity in class or for homework.

✱ Tip

Top margin

Chief Executive (also **Chief Executive Officer / CEO**)

the person in a company who has most power and authority and is responsible for managing its daily affairs under the authority of the board of directors

MD (**Managing Director**)

the member of a company's board of directors who is responsible for the running of a business on a daily basis

Ask students to think about the ideas expressed by these managers of big companies. What effect would their philosophy have on people?

➕ Additional activity

(weaker students)

Explain that as long as notes still make sense, you can omit: articles, subject pronouns, auxiliary verbs, and detailed information. You can reword to make a complex phrase much simpler. Ask students to underline the information about Nationwide in the article and tell you what words, expressions, and information have been omitted or simplified in the example notes.

Speaking

Go through the *Expressions* list with the students. Ask them to repeat the sentences after you, paying attention to pronunciation and intonation. You can use the recording to do this activity if you prefer.

Divide the class into pairs. Ask them to read their roles carefully. Remind them to use the expressions and question tags.

Reading

1 Ask students to read the list of companies and answer the questions.

> Shops: Asda, The Carphone Warehouse, Mothercare
> Factories: Cadbury Schweppes
> Work with money: Nationwide, KPMG

2 Tell students that all the companies are at the top of a list created by the *Sunday Times* newspaper. Then get them to read the article and make notes about the companies.

3 Get students to match the verbs with the words and phrases.

> 1 d   2 e   3 f   4 c   5 b   6 a

4 Go through the example with students, then ask them to discuss the other methods in the same way.

5 Ask students to work in groups and create their perfect company. This task requires students to use all the linguistic resources they have to negotiate together to arrive at a group decision. They can think of ideas other than the ones in the list, both from the unit and from brainstorming together.

6 Each group should nominate someone to present their ideas.

Business know-how

1 Ask students to work in pairs and discuss the questions.

> **Possible answers**
> **Similar** – it is a group of people working together; it has deadlines and projects; you get judged on the quality of your work; you work 'for' your teachers like you work for a boss, etc.
> **Different** – you don't get paid; you don't usually work in a team; you don't have a lot of autonomy, etc.

2 Ask students to work through the questions and answer them truthfully. This task is aimed at improving students' sense of autonomy and control.

3 This task invites students to learn how they can gain some control over how much satisfaction they get from their work. Ask them to work through the questions again and reflect on those where they said no.

➕ **Photocopiable activity**
Flexi-work
Go to p. 89 Teacher's Resource Book.

✳ Tip

Top margin
Go through the definitions with the students.

➕ Additional activity

(all levels)
Write these verbs on the board. Get students to find sentences with the verbs in the article. Then ask them to close their books. In groups, they should try to write truthful sentences about Lush using the verbs.

manufacture sell make believe buy own start launch set up consult

Company profile

Lush

1 Ask students to work in pairs and discuss the points.

2 Get students to read the article and answer the questions.

> ⚿ 1 organic, vegetarian cosmetics
> 2 Mark Constantine, his wife Mo, and Helen Anbrosen started by making products for the Body Shop twenty years ago. They then launched a company that went bankrupt, and in 1995 set up Lush.
> 3 Staff have a high opinion of Lush (they are on the *Sunday Times* list) and they have a laugh.
> 4 good value products, make a profit, the customer is always right

Writing

Ask students to read the instructions. Ask the class to tell you some of their ambitions for the future. Tell students to think of a job they would like. They should be realistic, and think of a job they are likely to do in their early career. This is not an exercise in thinking of an ideal job. Go through the example and ask students to write two paragraphs in class or for homework. Encourage students to refer back to their vocabulary notebooks to help them, and the job description exercise in Unit 6.

Project

Students can do this project individually or in pairs. Ask them to write notes about the company before they write their report. Write on the board these headings:

Type of company   What it does / manufactures   Size   Location   Profits
Why it is a good company to work for

Students can search on the company website and also use www.timesonline.co.uk and search for 100 Best Companies where there is an article about each listed company.

Checklist

Go through the checklist with the students. Get them to tell you which activities in the unit helped them practise each point. Ask the class if they need more practice in any of the areas.

Key words

Go through the list of words to check students' understanding.

12 Market research

Background

Companies need to understand what is happening in the marketplace in order to plan their business strategy. The collection of information to achieve this is called **market research**. There are two main methods of market research, **primary** and **secondary**.

Primary research, or **field research**, is for a specific purpose and provides new, previously unavailable data. This information is usually gathered by:

- face-to-face interviews – conducted in the street, workplace, or at people's homes, using scripted questions
- telephone interviews – using scripted questions
- printed questionnaires – in newspapers, magazines, or delivered in the mail
- the Internet – questionnaires delivered via email
- focus groups – groups of people respond to scripted questions. This provides more in-depth information than other techniques
- hall tests – people are invited into a room to test and express their opinions about products
- observation – trained 'people watchers' or ethnographers study people's reactions to products, advertisements, etc.

The great advantage of primary research is that it is targeted and the information is up to date. It is, however, time-consuming and expensive.

Secondary research, or **desk research**, is based on pre-existing data. This information is extracted from journals, government and company reports, surveys published by research organizations, etc. While cheaper and quicker than primary research, the information gathered is not always as relevant or up-to-the-minute.

In primary research, **questionnaires** can provide specific information that is vital to the success of a business venture. Questionnaires consist of long lists of questions designed to discover people's attitudes to existing products or services. The data they provide

- helps the company predict the product's performance
- gives a picture of the buying behaviour of customers
- reveals customer awareness of the product
- reveals customer attitudes to other existing or proposed products.

To produce the information that the company wants to find out (its objectives), questionnaires must be carefully constructed. The questions must be clear, easily understood, precise, and in a logical sequence. There are three main question types. They will either

- produce *Yes / No / Don't know* answers
- offer a scale of answers (*excellent, very good ... bad, etc.*)
- offer a range of answers (*Brand A / Brand B / Brand C*).

Companies will often engage a specialist company to collect and analyse the data for them.

Start up

1 Ask students to work in pairs, then round up at class level.

2 Ask students to discuss the questions in groups, then at class level.

> **⚷ Possible answers**
> 1 to understand their customers, to improve their products and services, to find out what new products and services to introduce
> 2 via interviews, focus groups, questionnaires
> 3 by giving samples, asking questions, showing products, asking customers to vote
> 4 by going to shops, trade fairs, asking customers

➕ Additional activity
(stronger students)
🎧 Ask students to listen again and answer these questions.
Listening 1: *What is wrong with the layout? Does the interviewee find shopping exciting?*
Listening 2: *What is wrong with the shop assistants? What is wrong with the layout? What could they do to make the shop more exciting?*

3 🎧 Go through the instructions, then play the recording for students to complete the table.

🔑	1	2		1	2
good choice	✓	✓	good service	✓	✗
high quality	✓	✓	exciting	✓	✗
high prices	✓	✗	clear layout	✗	✗
fashionable	✓	✗			

Reading

1 Ask students to use the above criteria to discuss a department store.

2 Ask students to read the research and do the matching exercise.

> 🔑 high prices = 75%   fashionable = 20%   good service = 50%
> good choice = 45%   clear layout = 35%   exciting = 5%

3 Get students to do the exercise in class or at home.

> 🔑 20% less than a quarter   35% about a third   45% less than half
> 52% just over half   75% three quarters

➕ Writing bank
Report
Go to p.62 Student's Book.

➕ Grammar test
Go to p.90 Teacher's Resource Book.

Language spot
First Conditional

Go through the grammar with the students. Ask them to find and underline the sentences in the report.

> 🔑 If customers believe the store sells high-quality goods, they will accept higher prices.
> Unless Melvilles updates its goods, it will lose out to its competitors.
> If more training is given, the staff will be able to provide better support to the customer.
> If consumers don't find a good selection, then they won't buy.
> If competing stores have better layouts, they will attract customers away from Melvilles.
> It will improve its position when it addresses the issues raised by this research.

Go through the Grammar reference with students or set it as homework.

1 Ask student to read and complete the advice in class.

> 🔑 1 choose   2 won't reflect   3 write   4 'll get   5 ask
> 6 will become   7 have   8 'll miss out   9 completes
> 10 'll find out

2 Ask students to complete the sentences then discuss them.

✳ Tip

Top margin

Ask students to close their books and then dictate the definition of *market research*. They can then check in their books.

After *Reading*, ask students to read the three quotes, then discuss what they mean with the whole class.

➕ Additional activity

(weaker students)

Ask students to find words in the article that mean:

A the way you act or behave (**behaviour**)

B to socialize with people (**hang out**)

E to look at something carefully (**go through**)

F to make somebody want to do something (**motivate**)

G having power or influence (**influential**)

➕ Additional activity

(stronger students)

🎧 Play the recording again and ask students to answer these questions:

1 Who employs Anna? (marketing companies)

2 Does she work alone? (no, she has a team)

3 What two techniques does she use in shops? (cameras and following people)

4 Who walks through shops quickly, men or women? (men)

5 Who reads labels more? (women)

6 How do companies use the information? (to improve their sales)

✳ Tip

Expressions

If there are too many expressions for weaker students, suggest they choose one or two to learn.

Reading

1 Ask students to read the title and guess what the article is about. Then get them to read it and match the headings with the paragraphs.

> 🔑 At home = F   Rubbish readers = E   Cool hunters = G   Shopping snoops = C
> Hanging out = B   Using technology = D

2 Get students to read the article again and answer the questions.

> 🔑 1 Because they study people's behaviour in their 'natural environment'.
> 2 To study why they make choices, how they really live
> 3 They follow them around the shop.
> 4 How people use technology
> 5 They go through their rubbish, stay in their houses, and watch them live.
> 6 They hang out with the teenagers and find influential leaders.

3 Ask students to work in groups and answer the questions.

> 🔑 **Possible answers**
> Observing people allows you to see real behaviour; when people talk they may not tell the truth, or be able to say what they want. Rubbish shows what you buy, eat, and throw away without even using.

Listening

🎧 Ask students to read the questions and speculate about the interview. Play the recording and get students to choose the correct answers.

> 🔑 1 b   2 a   3 b   4 c   5 b

Call centre

Asking polite questions

🎧 Ask students to read the dialogues, then listen and complete them.

> 🔑 1 wonder   2 could   3 Would   4 mind   5 Could
> 6 possibly   7 Would   8 able

Go through the *Expressions* list with the students. Ask them to repeat the sentences after you or after the recording.

Pronunciation

Polite requests

1 🎧 Explain that politeness depends not only on the expression you use, but also on the tone of voice and intonation.

2 🎧 Play the recording and ask students to decide if they are polite or rude.

> 🔑 2 R   3 R   4 P   5 R   6 P

Speaking

Go through the *Expressions* again and explain the activity. Students role-play boss and employee. Expressions the boss can use to refuse include *I'm sorry, but ..., I'm afraid that it's not possible.*

It's my job

1 Discuss with students whether they would like to be a market researcher.

2 Ask students to copy the table. Then get them to read about Matsuko Takahashi and complete the table.

O⟋ Training	Duties	Qualities and skills
professional qualification	write reports	like talking to people
		work independently
		work in a team

3 Ask students to read the text and answer the questions. In groups, students then discuss the situations and choose the following situation.

O⟋ **Possible answers**
1 survey, personal interviews
2 field trials
3 focus groups, observation
4 surveys, focus groups, chat rooms
5 surveys, observation, chat rooms

Business know-how

1 Ask the class to discuss the question and write their ideas on the board.

2 Ask students to read the tips and compare them with their ideas.

Writing

1 Ask students to write the questionnaire in class or for homework.

2 Ask students to ask and answer questions from the questionnaire in pairs.

Project

Ask students to work in pairs. Ask them to re-read the advice on writing questionnaires on p.85. Possible research areas: fast food, organic food, mobile phone use, cosmetics, reading habits, free-time activities.

Checklist

Go through the checklist with the students. Get them to tell you which activities in the unit helped them practise each point. Ask the class if they need more practice in any of the areas.

Key words

Go through the list of words to check students' understanding.

---

* Tip

Top margin
Ask students to brainstorm the skills and qualities a market researcher needs. Write them on the board.
Then go through the list. Did the students think of the same skills and qualities?

* Tip

scripted questions oral questions, written in advance

➕ Photocopiable activity
Understanding the market
Go to p.91 Teacher's Resource Book.

➕ Additional activity
(weaker students)
Students can write the questionnaire in pairs or groups.

➕ Additional activity
(stronger students)
Students can ask several people their questions and write a report on their results.

13 Bright ideas

Background

Many larger companies have a **Research and Development** (R & D) department. The common perception of R & D is that it is primarily concerned with the development of new products. However, as consumer preferences are constantly changing, the improvement of existing products to maintain and increase market share is of equal importance. Product improvements can range from ring-pull cans to smaller and faster PCs. New products are either the result of technological advances such as Sat Nav (satellite navigation for cars), or innovative new ideas such as Dyson's bagless vacuum cleaner.

In some industries, such as shoe or furniture manufacturing, there is little R & D, as the products change very little. In high-tech industries, where there is intense competition between companies and a constant demand for new products, investment is considerable. While most of the R & D budget is spent on developing products with clear sales potential, a large company may also allocate up to 10% of its budget to 'blue-sky' research. This is more speculative and is not expected to produce short-term results.

R & D can be a risky and expensive business. Some products, for example pharmaceutical products, will take years to develop. Companies also have to make predictions about what the economic situation will be like in the future, and the possibility of other technological breakthroughs which will fundamentally change the market. However, years of investment are no guarantee of success. 30% of new products fail in the laboratory and 60% during development.

The R & D department works very closely with the marketing department. While market research is crucial to the technical development of the product, it also impacts on design. The iMac and iPod are examples of products whose physical appearance has played a major role in their phenomenal success. Product development will typically follow this model:

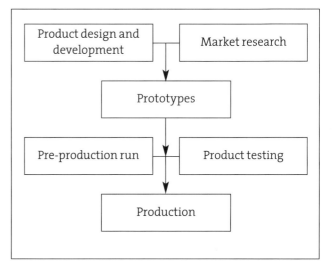

Some independent inventors with bright ideas may try to go it alone. The potential rewards are extremely high – but so are the chances of failure. Many try to sell their ideas to companies for them to develop. This way, the companies bear the burden of the development costs. And if the product is a success, even a low royalty will make the inventor wealthy.

Start up

1 Get students to read the list of inventions and think about the questions. Tell them that all the inventions have been recently invented by someone.

2 Get students to decide which of the inventions became successful products.

3 🎧 Get students to listen and note down the four successful products.

> ⚬━ inflatable cot   shoes for police dogs   multi-shirt clothes hanger
> trap to catch insects

✳ Tip

Encourage students to use the language of agreeing and disagreeing:
I think ..., I agree, I don't agree, What do you think?, I bet ..., I wouldn't be surprised if ...
They should also give reasons for their choices. Round up the ideas at class level and take a class vote. Ask them to say: *We thought ...*

➕ Grammar test

Go to p.92 Teacher's Resource Book.

➕ Additional activity

(weaker students)

● Dictate this text to students.
  Inflatable cot
  The inflatable cot was designed by a British inventor, Jo Bradford. Jo is an engineering graduate and the mother of three children. She thought of her invention when she was on holiday because she found it was difficult to take normal cots with her. Her invention only weighs four kilos and is easy to carry. She has received financial help to develop her product and has won business awards.
● Discuss the difficulties and rewards of being an inventor.

➕ Additional activity

(weaker students)

Ask the class as a whole questions about Jerry and Alicia.
When did Jerry live in London?
What was Jerry doing in 1997?
When did Alicia leave university?
What was Alicia doing in 1994?
What was Alicia doing in 2001?
What was Jerry doing in 2004?
When did Jerry do a business course?
When did Alicia start her own company?
When did Jerry move back to London?

Reading

1 Ask students to brainstorm in pairs, then round up at class level.

> **O⚷ Possible answers**
> typewriter, computer, printer, photocopier, filing cabinet, telephone, swivel chair, correction fluid, Post-it notes, stapler, hole puncher, paper clip

2 Ask students to look at the article headings and the pictures.

> **O⚷ QWERTY keyboard – Inventor**: Christopher Latham Sholes; **Date**: 1866; **How the invention happened**: Mechanical letters got stuck together when they were in alphabetical order, so he spaced commonly linked letters out.
> **Correction fluid – Inventor**: Bette Nesmith Graham; **Date**: 1951; **How the invention happened**: She used white paint to correct her mistakes and decided to make special fluid for the office.
> **Post-it notes – Inventor**: Art Fry; **Date**: 1970s; **How the invention happened**: He wanted bookmarks that didn't fall out. He used a colleague's unsuccessful adhesive.

Language spot
Past Continuous

Ask students to read the first rule and then find and underline three sentences in *Reading*. Then ask them to read the second rule. Go through the Grammar reference with students or set it as homework.

> **O⚷** One day (Bette) was typing at work when she made a mistake; Soon everyone was asking for her invention; While he was using bits of paper to mark pages in his song book, he thought of a great idea.

Ask students to look at the tables of the lives of Jerry and Alicia. and complete the sentences in class or for homework.

> **O⚷** 1 was studying   2 was studying, was living / lived   3 left
> 4 was travelling   5 got married   6 was living, was working
> 7 started, was working   8 started

Reading

1 Ask students to discuss the questions in groups.

2 Get students to read the article and match the headings to the paragraphs.

> **O⚷** 1 E   2 C   3 A   4 B   5 D

✳ Tip

Top margin

After *Reading*, students read the quotes. Discuss if the same principles apply in everyday life. Ask students what they think are the qualities and skills that Dyson has that means he is a successful inventor and businessman.

➕ Photocopiable activity
Research and development

Go to p.93 Teacher's Resource Book.

✳ Tip

Top margin

Ask students to read the Trevor Baylis quote. Do they feel that James Dyson's invention also reflects this philosophy? Is it also true for discoveries such as gravity? Can students think of any other inventors, inventions, or discoveries that support this idea?

➕ Additional activity

(stronger students)

Write these simplified sentences from the article on the board. Show students the use of the *–ing* form.

- *Inventors have to protect their ideas **by paying** to register a patent.*
- *He **started experimenting** and built ... Dyson never **stops thinking** about new ways ...*
- *He **started manufacturing** under his own name, **selling** affordable cleaners.*
- *He **spent** a further five years **developing** the product ...*

Ask students to complete these sentences with an *–ing* form of their own choice: *I think of new ideas by ..., I learn new words by ..., I do research by ..., To get fit, you should start ..., To get fit, you should stop ..., Last week I spent a lot of time ...*

3 Ask students to read the article again and answer the questions.

> **🗝 Possible answers**
>
> Paragraph A – Because it takes so long; it is expensive; you get rejected; there's no guarantee of success
>
> Paragraph C – Because they would have owned the product that caused a drop in Hoover sales; because he feels embarrassed not to have recognized a successful product
>
> Paragraph D – Because they cost a lot to develop; because Dyson only produced a few, and that costs more per unit
>
> Paragraph E – Because that way design goes hand in hand with engineering and doesn't come afterwards

Listening

1 Ask students to match the words with the definitions.

> **🗝** 1 E 2 D 3 F 4 B 5 C 6 A

2 🎧 Go through the questions with the students and get them to guess as much as possible about what the listening is going to be about. Then ask them to listen and decide if the sentences are true or false.

> **🗝** 1 F 2 T 3 T 4 F 5 F 6 T 7 T 8 F

9 to 5

Agreeing and disagreeing

1 🎧 Ask students to look at the picture and discuss what is happening. Then get them to listen and check their ideas.

2 🎧 Ask students to listen again and decide who is saying what.

> **🗝** 1 L 2 R 3 R 4 J 5 R 6 R 7 J

Speaking

Go through the *Expressions* list with the students. Ask them to repeat the sentences after you or after the recording. Students have to negotiate together using the expressions of agreeing and disagreeing. They should appoint someone to make notes and someone to present their proposal.

* Tip

Top margin

Ask students to read the Steve Jobs quotes. What do they tell you about his business philosophy?

➕ Additional activity

(*stronger students*)

Ask students to close their books. Dictate these sentence openings:

- *In 1976 the founders of Apple ...*
- *They sold the first computer for...*
- *It earned the company ...*
- *Their second-generation computer, Apple II, had ...*
- *In 1980 the company developed ...*
- *In the 1990s both founders ...*
- *In 1997 Steve Jobs ...*

Ask students to work in pairs and complete the sentences with correct information. The words don't have to be the same as the text. Then get them to open their books and check the information.

Company profile

Apple Computer Inc.

1 Ask students to work in groups and discuss the questions.

2 Get students to discuss Apple in pairs. Then round up on the board.

3 Ask students to read about Apple and answer the questions.

> 🔑 1 They were the fist home computers that were simple and easy to use. Apple II had on-screen graphics and a floppy disk drive.
>
> 2 The worst time was in the 1990s, when the company didn't keep up with the marketplace.
>
> 3 Steve Jobs focused on invention and innovation, and Apple moved into consumer electronics.
>
> 4 **Possible answers**
> easy to use and attractive computers, a way to download music easily

4 Get students to make notes about their hero, then talk about their heroes in groups.

Project

Students can use these websites to help them with the project:

www.trivialpursuit.com, www.inventors.about.com, www.ideafinder.com

They can either make a poster, write a report, or do a presentation to the class. Encourage them to use linkers and the *–ing* form in their report.

Business know-how

1 Ask students to answer the questions together in pairs.

2 Ask students to read and discuss the advice, then choose two activities.

Writing

Ask students to read about Richard Branson and answer these questions:

When did he start up in business? What famous artists did Virgin Records sign? What other businesses does he have? Why does the writer admire him?

Ask students to make notes about their hero and then to write a paragraph for a chat room. Encourage students to make a website with their texts on it.

Checklist

Go through the checklist with students. Get them to tell you which activities in the unit helped them practise each point. Ask the class if they need more practice in any of the areas.

Key words

Go through the list of words to check students' understanding.

14 Dealing with people

Background

A recent report in the UK suggests that anger in the workplace could have long-term consequences for companies. Anger at managers, colleagues, and customers is causing people to take time off from a stressful working environment. What could be considered as simply a personal 'emotional' issue actually has real economic side-effects. So anger management, whether dealing with one's own emotions or with angry colleagues or customers, is one of the soft skills which are now taught on training courses.

Research suggests that a person's **emotional intelligence** is more important than their **intellectual intelligence** (measured by their **IQ** or **intelligence quotient**). The higher a person's **EQ** (**emotional quotient**), the more successful he or she is likely to be. Emotional intelligence is a person's ability to understand their own emotions, and the emotions of others – and to use that knowledge to act appropriately. It is 'a way of recognizing, understanding, and choosing how we think, feel, and act. It shapes our interactions with others and our understanding of ourselves' (Freedman et al., *Handle with Care: Emotional Intelligence Activity Book*). It has been estimated that where IQ accounts for only 20% of the factors that determine whether a person will be successful or not, EQ accounts for 80%. It is clear from this why companies are spending much more time and energy on helping employees to develop the soft skills that can make them happier, and more effective, in their jobs.

The ability to get on with people, motivate oneself and others, manage conflicts, and deal with difficult situations reflects a person's EQ. Task-based work, for example fitting machinery parts on a car assembly line, does not require a great deal of emotional intelligence. However, as soon as one is in an office environment, working alongside colleagues, attending meetings, handling customers, and dealing with managers, then soft skills become far more important. Some of the skills taught on training courses include:

- Communication skills (including body language, effective listening, assertiveness, etc.)
- Anger management (including identifying feelings. recognizing anger, coping skills, etc.)
- Conflict resolution
- Getting along with co-workers
- Problem solving
- Time management
- Telephone skills
- Managing people.

* Tip

Go through the vocabulary of feelings and character with the class.

Start up

1 Ask students to work in pairs and discuss the questions.

2 Get students to do the quiz and read their profile.

3 Ask students to read the quiz in groups and analyse the different responses.

O—	1a	It is better to tell people when you are upset.
	1b	If something isn't really important, it is sometimes better not to say anything.
	1c	If you don't explain the problem, your working relationship may become difficult.
	2a	By asking questions, you show the caller that you appreciate their point of view.
	2b	By telling the caller it isn't your fault, you are creating a situation of conflict.
	2c	This does not deal with the situation.
	3a	If your colleagues have arranged a party, they clearly care. This deals with the situation maturely.
	3b	Going to the party is a good idea, but leaving early will look rude.

➕ Additional activity

(all levels)

Ask students to tell you how they would feel if

- they forgot their friend's birthday party
- they said something stupid
- their friend criticized them
- a famous person they admired died
- they had too much work to do
- a car they were in was going very fast.

➕ Grammar test

Go to p.94 Teacher's Resource Book.

3c Your colleagues will be confused and hurt by your behaviour.
4a By doing this, you can understand how to present yourself better.
4b Rewriting your CV may be a good idea, but in a calm way.
4c Being miserable is not productive at all.
5a It is best to communicate your feelings calmly.
5b Your irritation could affect your relationship, so it's better to talk.
5c You should deal with the situation face-to-face before involving your boss.

Language spot

Second Conditional

Ask students to read the rules and then look at all the Second Conditional sentences in the quiz.

Go through the Grammar reference with students or as homework.

1 Ask students to do the matching exercise.

> 🔑 1 e   2 a   3 d   4 f   5 c   6 b

2 Ask students to write sentences with their advice.

3 Ask students to work in pairs and choose two courses they would like to do.

✳ Tip

Give students an example from your own life, e.g. *I promised my daughter that I would take her to the cinema on her birthday, but I forgot that I had a training course that day and wouldn't get home on time. So I had to tell her that I couldn't take her. She was very angry with me. I felt guilty and upset. She said 'So your work is more important than your family!'. I decided that in future I would put my family first.*

➕ Additional activity

(weaker students)

In exercise 1 get students to think of one interaction instead of two. Ask them to write out their answers in full instead of making notes.

➕ Additional activity

(all levels)

Ask students to find two things in the article that surprised them or interested them and discuss them with their partner.

Reading

1 Ask students to work alone and make notes. They could think about interactions with their parents, siblings, friends, or colleagues.

2 Ask students to tell each other in pairs about their interactions. The listening student should ask questions and show interest.

3 Pre-teach: **IQ (Intelligence Quotient)**

Ask students to read the article and answer these questions orally:

What is EQ?   How does having a high EQ help in the workplace?

Then ask students to read the article again and answer the questions.

> 🔑 1 Because they involve emotions.   2 No, it doesn't; having an average IQ with a good emotional intelligence is a better indicator.   3 Your ability to understand and manage your emotions and manage your relationship with others.   4 Because they understand other people's feelings and are sensitive to other people's needs.   5 They benefit by getting higher performance levels and productivity from their staff and improved customer relations.

Vocabulary

Ask students to read the article again and find the words.

🔑 Verb	Noun	Verb	Noun
1 succeed	success	4 explain	explanation
2 improve	improvement	5 listen	listening
3 feel	feeling	6 perform	performance

Speaking

1 This activity is based on a psychological test used to get applicants to talk about themselves in a more revealing way than usual.

It's my job

1 Ask students if they ever go to listen to bands. Then ask students to work in pairs and brainstorm the responsibilities of a band manager.

2 Ask students to read the job profile and compare what Anna's responsibilities are to what they thought of.

> **⊶ Possible answers**
> take care of finances, apply for funding, manage the website, organize and promote gigs and tours, organize auditions, choose who to recruit, produce CDs, conduct

3 Ask students to discuss the question. Ask students what particular parts of Anna's job require Emotional Intelligence.

Call centre
Complaints

1 Ask students to work in pairs and discuss the questions.

> **⊶ Possible answers**
> A business needs to take complaints seriously and deal with each one individually. They should provide compensation for customers if they have done something wrong. If a company ignores complaints, customers will go elsewhere. They might go out of business if the complaints are serious. They will get a bad reputation. A complaint can help a company by pointing out problems, helping it improve its service and products. It can also get a good reputation as a listening company.

2 🎧 Play the recording and ask students to answer the questions.

> **⊶** 1 Because he has tried to contact Jonathan Andrews many times and left messages, and hasn't been called back
> 2 No, Anna stays calm
> 3 Anna offers to get Jonathan to call back tomorrow.

3 🎧 Go through the *Expressions*, then ask students to listen and tick the ones they hear.

> **⊶** I'm sorry about that.   What seems to be the problem?
> There seems to be a problem with ...   I'll look into it immediately.

4 🎧 Ask students to read through the dialogue, then listen and complete the gaps. Ask them to find more expressions from the *Expressions* list. (*I'm sorry to bother you but ... I'm going to ...*)

> **⊶** 1 speaking   2 help   3 bother   4 very   5 right
> 6 through   7 urgent   8 check   9 contact   10 gone

✳ Tip

Top margin

After doing the reading activities, ask students to read the quotes on p.98 and p.99 and discuss them in relation to emotional intelligence. Get them to choose the quote they like best.

➕ Photocopiable activity
Soft skills
Go to p.95 Teacher's Resource Book.

➕ Writing bank
Emails 6 – Complaining
Go to p.63 Student's Book.

➕ Additional activity
Ask students to read the profile again and answer these questions:
What does Anna call doing lots of jobs at the same time? (multi-tasking)
What qualities and skills does a band manager need? (efficient, a good writer, a good time manager, good at dealing with people)
What does Anna like best? (talking to different kinds of people, persuading people)
What is the most difficult thing for her? (delegating)

5 Ask students to read the tips and think of other advice, e.g. make notes of the problem, keep your promises, make a follow-up phone call to the client, etc.,

6 Ask students to find examples of the tips in the dialogue in exercises 2, 3, and 4.

Additional activity

(all levels)
One student thinks of someone in the group but doesn't say who it is. The rest of the group have to ask questions as in *Speaking* exercise 1 about that person and try to guess who it is.

✳ Tip

Top margin
Ask students to read the information on p.100 and discuss the implications for how companies should deal with complaints.

✳ Tip

Possible answer
Dear ABConline
I am writing to complain about a book I ordered two weeks ago.
The order number is 456-8790-003 and the title is *How to improve your EQ*.
You have unfortunately sent me the wrong book, *Adventures in Cinema*, and I have not received the book I ordered.
I would like you to deal with this problem urgently by sending me the correct book and collecting the incorrect book you have sent. If you don't do this within the next week, I expect a full refund.
I have already sent you two emails but you haven't replied. Could you please acknowledge this email.
Yours / Regards
Name

Speaking

Go through the *Expressions* list with the students. Ask them to repeat the sentences after you or after listening to dialogue 2.

Ask students to study their roles and make notes of the complaint they are going to make. Students can start with part of their complaint and then gradually tell the employee more about their problem. Ask students to use the tips and expressions from p.100.

Business know-how

1 Ask students to discuss the questions.

> **⊶ Possible answers**
> shouting, sulking, being irritable, being unreasonable
> **Advantages:** You communicate your problem and feel less angry.
> **Disadvantages:** You lose control; you may offend or upset people; you may get angrier.

2 Ask students to read the strategies and discuss which ones seem most useful.

Writing

1 Read through the situation with the students. At class level decide what you want to complain about and what you want ABConline to do.

2 Ask students to write an email complaining to ABConline. Suggest they use the expressions on p.100.

Project

Ask students to go online and try some personality tests, individually or in pairs, and to write notes about each test.

Checklist

Go through the checklist with the students. Get them to tell you which activities in the unit helped them practise each point. Ask the class if they need more practice in any of the areas.

Key words

Go through the list of words to check students' understanding.

15 Getting a job

Background

To get a job interview, to have a good interview, and then to follow it up, all require time, thought, and preparation. The successful job applicant will have to do most of the following:

- get work experience
- look for job advertisements, go to job fairs, etc.
- prepare a CV (Curriculum Vitae)
- write a letter of application
- find out about the company
- find out more about the market
- learn interview strategies (how to present oneself, analyse one's own strengths and weaknesses, prepare questions to ask at the interview, prepare answers to probable questions, etc.)
- write a follow-up letter

Assuming that the applicant gets as far as the interview, they need to do their homework as well as think about the *physical* impression they will make.

First impressions The majority of interviewers make their decisions within the first ten minutes. In fact, research reveals that dress, body language and facial expressions are more important for interviewers than what the applicant actually says. So interviewees should
- dress smartly
- be positive and friendly
- make eye contact.

Know the company In a recent survey, employers were asked to list interviewees' mistakes. The most common was demonstrating little or no knowledge of the company. This is particularly surprising when so much information is readily available on the Internet.

Be prepared Interviewees can anticipate many of the questions and so prepare their answers beforehand. Typical questions include: Why do you want this job? What are your strengths and weaknesses? Do you work well on your own? Where do you see yourself in five years' time?, etc.

Give examples Interviewers want to be sure that interviewees have the necessary skills to work well in their organization. Interviewees should give examples when they are asked to talk about when they have met a challenge, worked in a team, learnt new skills, etc. Without these, it won't be clear to the interviewers that they have the qualities and experience they claim.

✚ Additional exercise
(weaker students)
Ask students to tell you which expression goes with these situations:
- when you read a job advert and write a letter to an employee
- when you have a baby and take time off work
- when you decide to leave a job and write a letter or talk to your boss
- when you aren't well and you take time off
- when you are told you are going to have a better job
- when a company decides to ask you if you want to join them

Start up

Ask students to work in groups and discuss the questions.

Vocabulary

1 Ask students to look at the cartoons and match the captions and the pictures. Ask them to say which cartoon they think is the funniest.

> **О┱** a 3   b 6   c 5   d 4   e 2   f 1

2 Ask students to match the expressions with the cartoons.

> **О┱** be offered a job = 3   resign = 6   be off sick = 4   apply for a job = 5
> take maternity / paternity leave = 2   be promoted = 1

* Tip

appraisal
a meeting between an employee and their manager to discuss the quality of the employee's work and to plan future tasks

9 to 5

Talking about plans

1 🎧 Ask students to look at the picture. Is Lisa happy? Who is she speaking to? Play the recording and ask students to answer the questions.

> **⚷** 1 Because she's got a lot to do.
> 2 He is going to tidy the flat, do some shopping, and meet some friends, or stay in and watch a DVD. He may go hang-gliding with some friends.
> 3 She's got her appraisal on Monday.
> 4 She decides to go hang-gliding with Joe on Sunday.

2 🎧 Go through the *Expressions* with the students. Then play the recording and get them to tick the ones they hear.

> **⚷** What are your plans for the weekend?   I'll probably ...   I hope to ...   I may not ...   I might ...   I'm looking forward to it ...   I'm not looking forward to it.

3 🎧 Ask students to read through the dialogue before they listen. Then play the recording again and ask them to complete the gaps.

> **⚷** 1 'll   2 'll   3 may not   4 may   5 won't   6 might   7 won't
> 8 'll   9 might not   10 will

➕ Grammar test

Go to p.96 Teacher's Resource Book.

Language spot

will / won't, may / might

Get students to match the sentences with the rules.

> **⚷** a 3,6   b 1,4   c 2   d 5

Go through the Grammar reference with students or as homework.

Get students to write sentences about their future plans.

* Tip

In many varieties of English there are two /l/ sounds. The first one – clear 'l' – is often found in initial position, e.g. *led*. The back of the tongue is low in the mouth. In the second one – dark 'l' – the back of the tongue is high in the mouth. It is found after a vowel, 'j' or at the end of a word, e.g. *dull, film*. Dark 'l' is important for the pronunciation of *'ll*.

Pronunciation

Dark 'l'

1 🎧 Play the recording and ask students to listen carefully to the pronunciation of *'ll*. Play it again for students to repeat.

2 Ask students to talk about their plans for next week, making sure they pronounce the 'l' correctly.

Speaking

Go through the *Expressions* on p.103. Ask students to repeat the sentences after you. Get them to study their role carefully and then do the role-play. Encourage students to use *will / won't / may / might* and expressions from p.103.

✳ Tip

Top margin

Before doing exercise 2, ask students to read the facts about IKEA. Ask them if they would like to buy things from IKEA or work for them.

➕ Additional activity

(all levels)

Ask students to close their books and tell you what these numbers represent about IKEA. Divide the class into two teams, the first to get the correct answer wins a point.

- 160 million (copies of the catalogue)
- 200 (stores worldwide)
- 310 million (people visited stores last year)
- 76,000 (employees)
- £7.6 billion (annual global sales)
- 10,000 (products available)
- €46 billion Ingvar Kamprad (personal wealth)

Company profile

IKEA

1 Ask students to work in pairs and discuss their family's buying habits.

2 Ask students if they have ever heard of IKEA. Ask students to discuss the questions in exercise 2.

> **⊶ Possible answers**
> 1 the shopping experience, the fact that you can take the products home and build them yourself, the prices and designs, the range
> 2 It is positive because it encourages action and aims at low prices. It is negative because it makes the customer do the work.

Listening

1 Ask students to read the job advert and list the experience, skills, and qualities needed. Get them to compare their list with their partner.

> **⊶ Possible answers**
> experience – a similar job, or something at school that practised these skills
> skills – administration, using the phone, typing, using databases, writing emails, organizing events
> qualities – good at dealing with people, meeting deadlines, organizing information, friendly and outgoing

2 Ask students to look at the photos and ask them to describe the people. Ask them to decide which of the candidates they think the best might be.

3 🎧 Play the recording and get students to complete the table.

> **⊶ Paulette – experience**: has worked for several companies; **skills and qualities**: excellent computer and typing skills, enjoys office environment, likes getting the job done; **strengths**: works quickly, very efficient; **weaknesses**: works too hard; **possible comments**: a bit too confident and positive about herself
>
> **Antonio – experience**: has had a lot of summer jobs in travel agencies (dealt with questions on the phone, took bookings), has done factory jobs, edited school magazine; **skills and qualities**: enthusiasm, likes working with people, computer and telephone skills; **strengths**: enthusiasm, good at dealing with people, loves talking; **weaknesses**: can't drive; **possible comments**: not much experience, talks too much?
>
> **Tareq – experience**: does a similar job now (in a large company – he would prefer to work somewhere smaller); **skills and qualities**: well organized, reliable, enjoys working with people, good computer skills; **strengths**: good at working under pressure; **weaknesses**: finds it difficult to stop working; **possible comments**: not clear if he has all the necessary experience

+ Additional activity
(all levels)
Choose an interviewer and four candidates. Ask the class to be observers. Get the interviewer to do the role-play in front of the class. Then the class can vote for the best candidate.

+ Photocopiable activity
Interview techniques
Go to p.97 Teacher's Resource Book.

4 Ask students to decide in pairs which applicant they think is most suitable.

5 🎧 Play the recording and get students to make notes about the interviewer's comments.

> 🔑 **Paulette**: Excellent experience, hard-working, efficient; maybe doesn't have the people skills; also didn't ask any questions
> **Tareq**: Excellent experience, very reliable
> **Antonio**: Full of enthusiasm, a lot of good qualities, enjoys talking too much
> The interviewer chose Tareq.

Reading

1 Get students to read the article and match the mistakes with the advice.

> 🔑 a 10 b 1 c 9 d 7 e 4 f 6

2 Get students to discuss the behaviour in groups. Round up at class level.

Business know-how

1 Get students to brainstorm the question. Round up on the board.

2 Ask students to write their answers. Then get them to work in pairs and ask and answer the questions.

Speaking

Divide the students into groups of three – interviewer, candidate, and observer. Ask them to read and discuss the advert and candidate profile, then do the role-play. After each role-play ask the observer to share his / her notes with the other members of the group.

+ Writing bank
CVs
Go to p.59 Student's Book.

+ Writing bank
Letters 4 – Job applications
Go to p.64 Student's Book.

Writing

Ask students to complete the application form for themselves.

Project

Ask students to go to www.jobcentreplus.gov.uk. and choose a job to apply for. Ask them to write a paragraph saying why they would like the job and what skills and experience they have.

Checklist

Go through the checklist with the students. Get them to tell you which activities in the unit helped them practise each point. Ask the class if they need more practice in any of the areas.

Key words

Go through the list of words to check students' understanding.

Instructions for photocopiable activities

1 Introducing yourself

1 Give out the role cards and ask students to fill them in and make a name card before playing.

2 Go through the instructions with the class. Remind students to use the expressions on p.8, Student's Book. Then, either in large groups or as the whole class, students role-play being at a conference.

2 Departments

1 Ask students to read the people describing their jobs and write the names in the chart.

> ⊙╍ Research and Development – Lisa Papi
> Production – Dean Wilson
> Distribution – Ray Clarke
> Administration – Penny James
> Sales and Marketing – Mitsuko Saito
> Facilities – Filip Král
> IT – Agnès Laforgue
> Customer Care – Steven Baines
> Purchasing – David Lee
> Human Resources – Elena Morales
> Finance – Andrew Symonds

2 Ask students to read the text and think about the advantages and disadvantages in pairs.

3 Have the discussion at class level.

3 Greeting visitors

Divide the class into Student As and Student Bs. Give out the role cards and ask students to read them carefully in their groups. They should brainstorm what they will say for each topic. Then put the students in pairs (A and B) and ask them to do the role-play. Round up at class level and give students feedback on their performance.

4 Careers in sports

1 Ask students to look at the categories (the vertical list). Ask them to work in pairs and think of jobs for each category.

2 Discuss the questions at class level.

3 Ask students to read the web page and answer the questions.

4 Get students to discuss the statements in groups. Follow up: get them to write a paragraph about one of the statements.

5 Needs, wants, and preferences

1 Ask students to read the article and discuss the questions.

2 Get students to complete the table for each 'Need' individually.

3 Ask students to work in groups and compare what they have put.

4 Get students to work in groups and discuss the question.

6 Getting it right

1 Discuss the question at class level.

2 Ask students to read the article and answer the question, then to brainstorm changed products, e.g. chocolate packaging, mobile phones, etc.

3 Discuss the question at class level.

4 Ask students to read the text and answer the question.

5 Ask students to work in groups and try to imagine what the problems could be.

> ⊙╍ 1 In Spanish, 'No va' means 'It doesn't go'.
> 2 It becomes 'Schweppes Toilet Water' in Italian.
> 3 In Spanish, this translates as 'Fly naked'.
> 4 In German, 'Mist' means 'Waste that comes out of the back of animals'.
> 5 This slogan became 'Eat your fingers off'.

6 Ask students to brainstorm foreign brands that are successful in their country.

7 Careers fair

Divide the class into Student As and Student Bs. Give out the role cards and ask students to read them carefully in their groups. They should brainstorm what they will say for each topic. Then put the students in pairs (A and B) and ask them to do the role-play. Round up at class level and give students feedback on their performance.

8 Promoting products

1 Ask students to read about USPs and then work in pairs to decide on the USPs for the products.

2 Ask students to think about how adverts work. Get them to remember the aspects of advertising in the article on p.48.

3 Get students to read the article and compare their ideas with it.

4 Ask students to match AIDA with the sentences.

5 Ask students to work in groups and create a magazine advertisement. First get students to choose the product. Provide magazines for students to get their ideas from.

6 Get students to put the adverts up around the class. Then they should go round in pairs and discuss each one. Round up opinions at class level.

9 Dressing for work

1 At class level, brainstorm typical business outfits.

2 Ask students to complete the table.

3 Ask students to write descriptions of the pictures.

4 Get students to work in groups and discuss the questions.

10 Going online

1 Ask students to read the article. Get them to discuss the questions in groups and then round up ideas at class level.

2 Ask students to read the article and answer questions 1 and 2 individually. Then get them to work in groups to discuss question 3 in groups.

11 Flexi-work

1 Get students to write down advantages and disadvantages in pairs.

2 Ask students to go back through their ideas and label the points.

3 Ask students to read the article and underline the ideas they thought of. Ask them to add new ideas to their list.

4 Discuss the questions at class level.

12 Understanding the market

1 Ask students to read the article and label the techniques.

> 🔑 National newspapers = S
> Personal interviews = P
> Observation = P
> Trade press = S
> Printed questionnaire = P
> Online questionnaire = P
> Focus groups = P
> Hall tests = P
> Official reports = S
> Telephone interviews = P
> Company reports = S
> Local newspapers = S

2 Ask students to discuss the benefits and disadvantages.

3 Ask students to do the task in groups. Get them to present their ideas to the class.

13 Research and development

1 Ask students to read the article and discuss the questions.

2 Ask students to look at the products and guess what decade they came from.

> 🔑 pocket calculator – 1971
> Playstation – 1994
> DVDs – 1996
> disposable lighter – 1971
> microwave oven – 1947
> suntan lotion – 1936
> laptop computer – 1983
> miniskirt – 1965
> superglue – 1956
> trainers – 1947
> CDs – 1980

3 Ask students to work in groups and brainstorm ideas.

4 Round up at class level and vote for the top products.

14 Soft skills

1 Get students to do the quiz individually.

2 Get students to compare their answers in pairs. At class level discuss these skills and how students can develop them.

15 Interview techniques

1 Ask students to read the article and match the questions.

> 🔑 A3 B5 C4 D1 E2

2 Ask students to discuss the questions in pairs.

3 Discuss the advert with the class and brainstorm the qualities needed.

4 In groups get students to role play a job interview, using the questions on this handout and on p.106, Student's Book.

1 Grammar test

1 Complete the sentences with the correct form of the Present Simple.

1 They *spend* (spend) a long time working at their computers.
2 The company _____ (not, allow) employees to surf the Net.
3 Julie often _____ (arrive) late for meetings.
4 David _____ (get) about 30 cmails a day.
5 We _____ (not, sell) our goods in the Far East.
6 They _____ (prefer) working in an open-plan office.
7 Alessandra _____ (not, have) a busy schedule next week.
8 Lars _____ (study) English for an hour every evening after work.
9 He _____ (send) over 50 emails a day.
10 I _____ (not, have) a busy schedule this week.

2 Complete the questions using the Present Simple.

1 **A** *Are you* a sales representative?
   B No, I'm not. I'm a personal assistant.
2 **A** What time _____ work?
   B She usually starts work at 8.45.
3 **A** Where _____?
   B He works in central Berlin.
4 **A** _____ in a team?
   B Yes, they enjoy working in a team.
5 **A** How long _____ for lunch?
   B They take an hour.
6 **A** What _____?
   B My main responsibilities are meeting clients and negotiating contracts.
7 **A** What kind of computer _____?
   B Andrew uses an iMac.
8 **A** When _____ your holiday?
   B We take it in August.
9 **A** _____ working long days?
   B No, Ella doesn't mind working long days.
10 **A** What time _____ in the evening?
   B I finish at 6.30.

3 Write sentences about Pawel in your notebook.

	travel	deal with people	work in a team	use technology	do research
like	✓				
not like				✓	
not mind			✓		
hate					✓
good at		✓			

EXAMPLE
He likes travelling.

1 Introducing yourself

1 You are going to attend a conference with two colleagues. Work in groups of three and complete your role cards.

- Choose the name of your company.
- Choose your name. Either use your own name or invent another.
- Choose the job you do for the company. Look again at p.5 or choose a different one.
- Note two or three of your responsibilities.
- Now make a name card or a label so people know who you are.

2 Now you are at the conference. It's important to talk to the other conference-goers. Try to keep the conversations going!

- Introduce yourself to someone from another company.
- Find out who that person is, who they work for, and what they do.
- Introduce that person to one of your colleagues.
- Continue until your teacher stops you.

Name

Company

Job

Responsibilities

✂ -

1 You are going to attend a conference with two colleagues. Work in groups of three and complete your role cards.

- Choose the name of your company.
- Choose your name. Either use your own name or invent another.
- Choose the job you do for the company. Look again at p.5 or choose a different one.
- Note two or three of your responsibilities.
- Now make a name card or a label so people know who you are.

2 Now you are at the conference. It's important to talk to the other conference-goers. Try to keep the conversations going!

- Introduce yourself to someone from another company.
- Find out who that person is, who they work for, and what they do.
- Introduce that person to one of your colleagues.
- Continue until your teacher stops you.

Name

Company

Job

Responsibilities

2 Grammar test

1 Complete the sentences with the Present Simple or the Present Continuous.

1 Carmen *is working* (work) in the Madrid office this week.

2 What _____ (your department, do)?

3 We _____ (not, achieve) enough sales this month.

4 They _____ (want) to send me on a training course.

5 Facilities _____ (organize) the maintenance of the building.

6 **A** What _____ (Sebastian, do) these days?

   B He _____ (do) a two-year business course.

7 Max _____ (never, miss) a deadline.

8 My boss _____ (be) really stressed at the moment.

9 Who _____ (you, write) that letter to?

10 She often _____ (fly) to Warsaw to visit the head office.

2 Read the email and underline the correct form of the verbs.

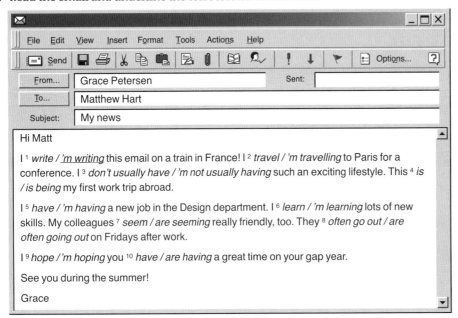

> File Edit View Insert Format Tools Actions Help
>
> Send
>
> From... Grace Petersen   Sent:
> To... Matthew Hart
> Subject: My news
>
> Hi Matt
>
> I ¹ *write / 'm writing* this email on a train in France! I ² *travel / 'm travelling* to Paris for a conference. I ³ *don't usually have / 'm not usually having* such an exciting lifestyle. This ⁴ *is / is being* my first work trip abroad.
>
> I ⁵ *have / 'm having* a new job in the Design department. I ⁶ *learn / 'm learning* lots of new skills. My colleagues ⁷ *seem / are seeming* really friendly, too. They ⁸ *often go out / are often going out* on Fridays after work.
>
> I ⁹ *hope / 'm hoping* you ¹⁰ *have / are having* a great time on your gap year.
>
> See you during the summer!
>
> Grace

3 Complete the dialogues using the correct form of the verbs. Use short forms.

A What ¹ *do you do* (you, do)?

B I ² _____ (work) for a computer software company.

A What ³ _____ (you, do) at the moment?

B I ⁴ _____ (develop) a new computer game.

A Where ⁵ _____ (be) Alex?

B He ⁶ _____ (drive) Leonardo to the airport.

A Why ⁷ _____ (he, see) his manager?

B They ⁸ _____ (talk) about his promotion.

A What ⁹ _____ (Ben and Katie, do)?

B Ben ¹⁰ _____ (talk) to the Sales Manager and Katie ¹¹ _____ (be, not) in the office today. She ¹² _____ (visit) clients.

2 Departments

1 Which departments do these people work for? Complete the chart.

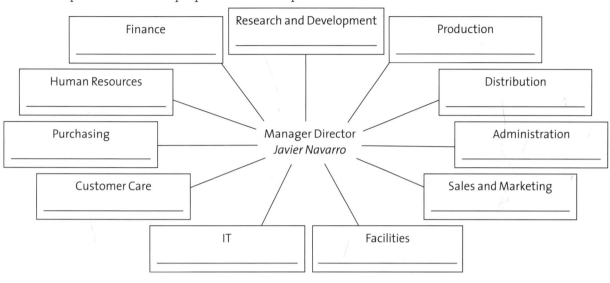

❚❚ This is a busy time of
the year because we're
producing the annual
accounts. **❚❚**
Andrew Symonds

❚ We're doing health and
safety checks around the
building this month. **❚❚**
Filip Král

❝❝ We make sure that all our goods are properly
packed and labelled before they are dispatched. **❞❞**
Ray Clarke

❝❝ This week we're installing new virus
protection on our whole system. **❞❞**
Agnès Laforgue

❚❚ We check the quality of the
product at each stage of the
manufacturing process. **❚❚**
Dean Wilson

❝❝ We notify our staff if there are
promotion opportunities. **❞❞**
Elena Morales

❚❚ At the moment we're designing an
exciting range of new products. **❚❚**
Lisa Papi

❚ We're dealing with lots of enquiries at
the moment. It's a busy time! **❚**
Steven Baines

❝❝ We maintain good relations
with our suppliers. **❞❞**
David Lee

❝❝ We produce and distribute publicity materials
such as catalogues and brochures. **❞❞**
Mitsuko Saito

❚ We do everything from organizing meetings to
making travel arrangements. It's non-stop! **❚**
Penny James

2 Read the text and answer the question. What are the
advantages and disadvantages of departments

- for the company?
- for employees?

Advantages	Disadvantages
Employees are members of a team.	*Departments don't communicate with each other.*

Businesses often choose
to specialize in one activity
and concentrate on doing
what they are good at.
In larger business
organizations, formal groups or departments
also specialize in
particular activities. The
employees within these
departments focus on
specific tasks.

3 What do you think? Is it better to work

- in a small company and learn lots of different jobs?
- in a large company, in one department, and specialize?

3 Grammar test

1 Write the Past Simple forms of these verbs.

1 study   _studied_   4 travel _____   7 apply _____   10 work _____

2 take _____   5 read _____   8 go _____   11 buy _____

3 come _____   6 stand _____   9 plan _____   12 find _____

2 Complete the sentences using the Past Simple.

1 Thomas _decided_ (decide) to stay in a hotel near the airport.

2 bmi _____ (start) as a flying school in 1948.

3 _____ (Louise, pack) an alarm clock?

4 I _____ (miss) the flight because I overslept.

5 We _____ (meet) at the sales conference last year.

6 Which proposal _____ (they, choose)?

3 Make sentences using the correct form of the Past Simple.

1 What / do / yesterday?

What did you do yesterday?

2 We / wait / at the station for more than two hours but the train / not arrive.

_____

3 Mr Janssen / sign / the contract yesterday?

_____

4 She / try / to call on her mobile but she / not able / to get a signal.

_____

5 I / forget / to buy the tickets.

_____

6 Why / Melissa / not apply / for that job?

_____

4 Complete the dialogue with the correct form of the verbs. It's Monday morning in the office.

watch	not serve	go	finish	sleep	be
not clean	~~have~~	not be able to	do	not work	be

A ¹_Did you have_ a successful trip?

B Yes, thanks. The meeting ² _____ really well. We even ³ _____ early on Friday afternoon.

A And how ⁴ _____ the hotel?

B The air conditioning in my room ⁵ _____. They ⁶ _____ my room. I ⁷ _____ get internet access. And they ⁸ _____ food in the restaurant after nine o'clock.

A That's terrible!

B But the worse thing ⁹ _____ the noise. The people in the next room ¹⁰ _____ TV until 3 o'clock every morning.

A So what ¹¹ _____ over the weekend?

B I ¹² _____ !

3 Greeting visitors

You are meeting a visitor from another country. Before you meet, decide together:

- who you are ● where you are ● your jobs ● the reason for the visit

1 Role-play your meeting at the airport.

Expressions
Hello, are you ... ? I'm ...
It's good to meet you.
Did you have a good journey? / How was your flight?
Would you like something to drink?
Can I help you with your luggage?
Shall we go straight to your hotel / the office / the restaurant?

2 Role-play your conversation at a restaurant.
It's important to be able to make conversation and to maintain a relaxed atmosphere – you can't talk about work all the time. This is where 'small talk' comes in. Be prepared to talk about:

- the weather at home
- your family
- your home
- your home town or city
- sport and the news
- the weather in your visitor's country
- your visitor's family
- your visitor's home
- your visitor's home town or city.

Try to keep the conversation going as long as possible!

✂ -

You are a visitor from another country. Before you meet your host, decide together:

- who you are ● where you are ● your jobs ● the reason for the visit

1 Role-play your meeting at the airport.

Expressions
Hello, are you ... ? I'm ...
It's good to meet you.
The journey was fine. / Not too bad. / It was pretty awful. There was ...
Could we have a coffee / something to eat before we leave?

2 Role-play your conversation at a restaurant.
It's important to be able to make conversation and to maintain a relaxed atmosphere – you can't talk about work all the time. This is where 'small talk' comes in. Be prepared to talk about:

- the weather at home
- your family
- your home
- your home town or city
- sport and the news
- the weather in the place you're visiting
- your host's family
- your host's home
- the place you're visiting.

Try to keep the conversation going as long as possible!

4 Grammar test

1 Write the questions and answers. Use the Past Simple or the Present Perfect.

1 **A** what time / arrive / this morning? _What time did you arrive this morning?_

B I / get / here / at about quarter past nine _____

2 **A** you / ever / consider / a career in sport? _____

B yes / . / in fact / I / work / in a gym / two years ago _____

3 **A** what / do / at the training course / yesterday? _____

B we / learn / how to run effective meetings _____

4 **A** they / ever / go / to the USA before? _____

B yes / . / they / go / a couple of years ago _____

2 Complete the conversation using the correct form of the verbs. Use short forms.

Richard OK, Barbara, I just want to check on your progress here. When ¹ _did your work experience begin_ (your work experience / begin)?

Barbara I ² _____ (start) at the end of June.

Richard So you ³ _____ (be) here for nearly two months now. OK, what different aspects of the job ⁴ _____ (cover)?

Barbara Well, I ⁵ _____ (work) in reception and I ⁶ _____ (answer) the phones. I ⁷ _____ (also, help) update the database.

Richard ⁸ _____ (work) in the gyms at all?

Barbara Actually, I ⁹ _____ (be) in the gym last week. I ¹⁰ _____ (follow) some instructors for a day and they ¹¹ _____ (show) me the different exercise routines. I really ¹² _____ (enjoy) it.

Richard ¹³ _____ (see) any other classes?

Barbara I ¹⁴ _____ (watch) an aerobics class last week.

Richard What other things ¹⁵ _____ (you, want) to do before you go back to university?

Barbara Well, ¹⁶ _____ (not work) in the pool. I'd love to do that.

3 Look at the Past Simple and Present Perfect verbs. Tick (✓) the correct ones, cross (✗) the wrong ones and correct the sentences.

1 ✗ They ~~have won~~ the sports brand of the year award in 2005. *(won)*

2 ☐ Have you ever dreamed of managing a major football club?

3 ☐ I put on a lot of weight. I must go to the gym!

4 ☐ How many sports events have you been to so far this year?

5 ☐ He hasn't got hands-on experience and he didn't run a business before.

6 ☐ When I was 18 I have trained in sports management.

4 Careers in sports

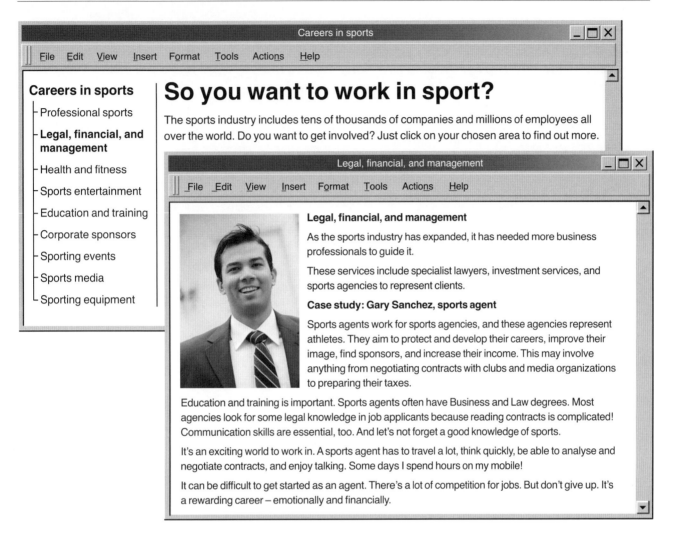

So you want to work in sport?

Careers in sports

- Professional sports
- **Legal, financial, and management**
- Health and fitness
- Sports entertainment
- Education and training
- Corporate sponsors
- Sporting events
- Sports media
- Sporting equipment

The sports industry includes tens of thousands of companies and millions of employees all over the world. Do you want to get involved? Just click on your chosen area to find out more.

Legal, financial, and management

As the sports industry has expanded, it has needed more business professionals to guide it.

These services include specialist lawyers, investment services, and sports agencies to represent clients.

Case study: Gary Sanchez, sports agent

Sports agents work for sports agencies, and these agencies represent athletes. They aim to protect and develop their careers, improve their image, find sponsors, and increase their income. This may involve anything from negotiating contracts with clubs and media organizations to preparing their taxes.

Education and training is important. Sports agents often have Business and Law degrees. Most agencies look for some legal knowledge in job applicants because reading contracts is complicated! Communication skills are essential, too. And let's not forget a good knowledge of sports.

It's an exciting world to work in. A sports agent has to travel a lot, think quickly, be able to analyse and negotiate contracts, and enjoy talking. Some days I spend hours on my mobile!

It can be difficult to get started as an agent. There's a lot of competition for jobs. But don't give up. It's a rewarding career – emotionally and financially.

1 Work in pairs. Try to write three jobs for each category of sports career in the 'Careers in sports' list above.

EXAMPLE
Professional sports – footballer, tennis player, basketball player

2 Would you like a career in sport? Which area are you interested in? Why?

3 Read the web page and answer the questions.
1. What do sports agencies do?
2. What skills and qualifications does a sports agent need?
3. What kind of activities does the job involve?
4. Why is it a difficult career to get into?

4 What do you think? Agree or disagree with the following statements.
- Sports agents are bad for sport.
- Corporate sponsors are good for sports stars and clubs.
- With cable and satellite TV, there is now no reason to attend live sporting events.
- Professional athletes make too much money.
- Sport is another branch of entertainment, like music or films.

5 Grammar test

1 Complete the email using the Present Continuous.

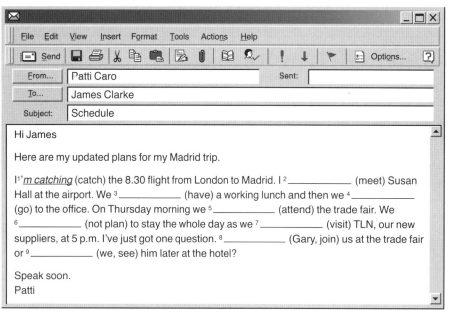

Hi James

Here are my updated plans for my Madrid trip.

I ¹ *'m catching* (catch) the 8.30 flight from London to Madrid. I ² _____ (meet) Susan Hall at the airport. We ³ _____ (have) a working lunch and then we ⁴ _____ (go) to the office. On Thursday morning we ⁵ _____ (attend) the trade fair. We ⁶ _____ (not plan) to stay the whole day as we ⁷ _____ (visit) TLN, our new suppliers, at 5 p.m. I've just got one question. ⁸ _____ (Gary, join) us at the trade fair or ⁹ _____ (we, see) him later at the hotel?

Speak soon.
Patti

2 How do Marie and Alan intend to change their lives? Complete the sentences.

Marie's New Year Resolutions
- *learn how to use PowerPoint*
- *don't send more than ten text messages a day*
- *leave work before 7*
- *apply for a new job*

Alan's New Year Resolutions
- *improve my sales technique*
- *set clearer targets*
- *leave work before 7*
- *apply for a new job*

1 Marie is going to learn how to use PowerPoint.
2 Alan _____
3 Marie _____
4 Alan _____
5 They _____
6 They _____

3 Complete the sentences with the correct forms of the Present Continuous or *be going to*.

1 As you can see from the figures, our sales to China *are decreasing* (decrease) due to problems with our distributors.

2 _____ (you, do) anything tomorrow afternoon?

3 Unfortunately, the graph shows that levels of customer satisfaction _____ (fall).

4 Paola _____ (not, like) this customer feedback.

5 _____ (she, take) the job in Paris?

6 I'm afraid I _____ (meet) a sales rep at 3.30.

7 I _____ (not, write) any more letters today.

8 The figures show that costs _____ (not, increase) at the same rate.

5 Needs, wants, and preferences

1 Read the text and discuss the questions.

1 Why do you think it is important for companies to know their customers' key expectations?

2 What are your key expectations for a mobile phone?

3 What is the difference between a **need** and a **preference**?

Trying to keep the customers satisfied

We are all consumers – and we are all different. When you buy a new mobile phone, you have a set of expectations. You may want it to be small and attractive. Or you may want it to have internet access. Or you may simply want it to be cheap and easy to use. If the product doesn't meet your key expectations, you will be dissatisfied. And the next time you want a new mobile phone, you will probably buy it from a different manufacturer.

Every customer has needs, wants, and preferences.

- A **need** is something you require. It could be goods or services. (a dictionary)

- A **want** is what it must be like. It is a general description of what you require. (bi-lingual, with business terminology)

- A **preference** is your personal choice, it's the ideal product. You may or may not find it. (not too expensive)

2 Imagine you have the following needs and complete the table.

	Need *I need ...*	Want *It must be ...*	Preference *I would prefer ...*
a laptop computer			
a pair of trainers			
a personal stereo			
a fast-food restaurant			
a pair of trousers			
a car			
a flight to London			
a TV			

3 Work in groups and compare your wants and preferences.

- Are they similar or different?
- Would they be the same for different age groups? Or for men or women?

4 Work in groups and discuss the question:

Imagine you are a manufacturer of laptop computers. Which key customer expectations would you choose to meet?

6 Grammar test

1 Complete the sentences with *must* or *mustn't* and the verbs below.

be
avoid
take off
stand
arrive
~~put~~
stare
eat

Top *travel tips*

1 In Austria, you *mustn't put* you're your hands on your lap during a meal. (✗)

2 In Denmark, you _____ on time for dinner invitations. (✓)

3 In the UK, you _____ at people in public. (✗)

4 In the Middle East, you _____ your shoes when you enter someone's home. (✓)

5 In Japan, you _____ strong displays of emotion in public. (✓)

6 In Germany, you _____ punctual when you have a business meeting. (✓)

7 In Pakistan you _____ with your left hand. (✗)

8 In the USA, you _____ at least a metre from other people when you are talking. (✓)

2 Complete the sentences with the correct forms of *mustn't* or *don't have to*.

1 You *mustn't* smoke inside the building.

2 We have a relaxed dress code. Our male staff _____ wear suits and ties.

3 They _____ make personal phone calls in the office.

4 You _____ be late for the meeting. It's extremely important.

5 You _____ be mad to work here, but it helps.

6 We _____ forget to take the PowerPoint presentation!

7 Lisa _____ finish the report today. She can finish it tomorrow.

8 You _____ tell Karl that you are planning to leave.

3 Complete the sentences using the correct forms of *must*, *have to*, and the words in brackets. Sometimes more than one form is possible.

1 *Does Amanda have to take* (Amanda / take) any more examinations before she qualifies?

2 _____ (you / not / say) anything to Beatrice. She doesn't know.

3 _____ (I / deal with) customer complaints in my job. Fortunately, there aren't too many!

4 _____ (I / get) in touch with our suppliers tomorrow.

5 _____ (you / leave) home early to get here on time today?

6 _____ (he / remember) to follow the instructions next time. It's absolutely essential.

7 _____ (applicants / not / have) work experience.

8 _____ (we / go) on a training course last week.

9 A _____ (you / work) in the office every day?

B No, I don't, because I can work from home, but _____ (I / be) contactable by phone.

10 _____ (visitors / not / leave) their cars in front of the building. They'll get a parking ticket!

4 In your notebook, write ten rules for your ideal work place.

1 You have to be smart, but you don't have to wear formal clothes.

2 You mustn't work at weekends – it's bad for you.

6 Getting it right

1 Companies often try to improve their products. Why do you think they do this? What can possibly go wrong?

2 Now read the first article and answer the questions.
- Why wasn't New Coke successful?
- Think of other products that have changed. Were the changes always improvements?

3 What problems could a company have when it promotes its products in foreign countries?

4 Now read the second article. What was the problem with the Electrolux slogan?

5 Work in groups. The following products had problems in their target markets. Discuss possible reasons.
1 General Motors launched the Chevy Nova in South America.
2 Schweppes started selling Tonic Water in Italy.
3 American Airlines promoted its first-class leather seats to the Mexican market with the slogan, 'Fly in leather'.
4 Clairol introduced the Mist Stick (a device for hair care) to Germany.
5 Kentucky Fried Chicken's 'finger lickin' good' slogan in China.

6 Which foreign brands are successful in your country?

Know your customer

Companies have to understand the culture that surrounds their own established products. Their customers expect certain levels of quality, taste, or image. Coca-Cola decided to change the formula for its famous drink and created New Coke. Its market research suggested that it was very popular. Unfortunately, when they launched it in 1985, they had a disaster on their hands. The classic drink was an American icon. People didn't want any changes. So the sales of New Coke fell – and the company soon returned to its classic formula and classic taste.

Check your language

Companies must also be aware of foreign cultures when they launch new products. They have to understand local sensibilities and tastes – and the importance of language! The Swedish company Electrolux launched its vacuum cleaners in the US with the slogan 'Nothing sucks like Electrolux'. Good suction is an excellent quality in a vacuum cleaner. Unfortunately, in American slang, if something 'sucks', then it is awful.

7 Grammar test

1 Complete the sentences with *should* or *shouldn't* and the verbs in brackets.

> ## *How to* **maintain a successful brand**
>
> Starbucks is one of the most successful brands of the last decade. Here are some of its secrets that other brands could learn.
>
> 1 You *should try* (try) to exceed your own expectations.
> 2 You _____ (have) strong values and you _____ (use) them to help you make decisions.
> 3 You _____ (forget) that every detail is important.
> 4 You _____ (keep on) trying to innovate and do new things – but you _____ (change) the core of what you do.
> 5 You _____ (get) involved with local communities and community projects.

2 Write the questions using *should*.

1 (you / think / I / take / business cards to the trades fair?)
   Do you think I should take business cards to the trades fair?

2 (what / you / think / we / take?)
   _____

3 (where / I / put / the files?)
   _____

4 (you / think / I / ask / for a pay rise?)
   _____

5 (how long / you / think / she / stay at the conference?)
   _____

6 (who / they / send the documents to?)
   _____

3 Write two pieces of advice for each of these problems. They can be negative or positive.

1 I always have too many things to do and I never finish any of them.
   You should make a list of things you have to do and work through them.
   You shouldn't try to do everything at the same time.

2 I'm going to a careers fair next week and I don't know what to wear.

3 I have a job interview tomorrow and I'm really nervous.

4 I always arrive late for work in the morning.

5 My boss doesn't appreciate me. I don't think she understands all the work I do for her.

6 I share an office with two other people. They spend a lot of the day talking to each other. I find it very difficult to concentrate on my work.

7 I keep losing my mobile. I never know where it is.

8 When I go home I can't stop thinking about work. It's taking over my private life!

4 How could you be a better student? Write eight sentences in your notebook.
   1 I should organize my time better.
   2 I shouldn't listen to dance music while I'm working.

7 Careers fair

Student A

You are a student. You are a visitor to a careers fair. You are interested in working in import / export.

1 Before you start:

a Think about you.
- What are you studying?
- Why are you interested in import / export?
- What are your strengths and weaknesses? (*I'm good at ..., I like ..., I'm not keen on ...*)
- Do you have any experience? (*I've worked ... / done ...*)

b Think about what questions to ask about the company. Find out
- what products the company imports / exports
- which countries it works with
- if it has a training programme for new employees
- if it offers work experience internships.

c Make some simple business cards on pieces of paper with your name and contact details.

2 Now go to the careers fair. Don't forget to
- introduce yourself
- take notes
- ask for a business card
- give your business card.

3 After the fair. Which companies are you interested in? Why?

- -

Student B

You are working on a company stand at a careers fair. You work for an import / export company.

1 Before you start:

a Write the name of your company on a sheet of paper and display it clearly on your desk.

b Think about your company.
- What products do you import / export?
- Which countries do you work with?
- Do you have training programmes for new employees?
- Do you offer work experience internships?

c Make some simple business cards on some pieces of paper. Write the name of your company, your name, and contact details.

d Think about what to ask the visitor. Find out:
- what they are studying (*What ... ?*)
- why they are interested in your company (*Why ... ?*)
- the visitor's strengths and weaknesses (*What ... ?*)
- if the visitor has any relevant experience (*Do you have ... ?*)

2 Now work at your company stand at the careers fair. Don't forget to ask for a business card.

3 After the fair. Which visitors to your stand are you interested in? Why?

8 Grammar test

1 Write the comparative and superlative forms of these adjectives.

1	easy	*easier*	*the easiest*
2	competitive		
3	big		
4	effective		
5	far		
6	costly		
7	bad		
8	interesting		
9	simple		
10	hot		

2 Complete the conversation with the comparative and superlative forms.

A OK, so what's the [1]*best* (good) way to promote our new range of products?

B Well, [2]_____ (effective) way to promote is definitely on TV.

C But that's [3]_____ (expensive) option, too! We only have a small budget.

B Well, radio advertising is [4]_____ (cheap).

C It also reaches a [5]_____ (small) audience.

A That's true, but it is [6]_____ (exciting) than print advertising.

C We should consider billboards. They are one of [7]_____ (fast) growing segments in advertising. They're one of [8]_____ (cheap) ways to reach a mass audience.

A Well, I think we agree that a TV campaign is [9]_____ (good) option. And we should make our online store [10]_____ (easy) to use, too.

3 Write the questions using superlative adjectives, then write your own answers.

1 (what / bad / day of the working week?)

What's the worst day of the working week? Monday is the worst day because it is difficult to get up!

2 what / good / advertisement / you / ever / see?

_____

3 who / famous / business person in your country?

_____

4 what / difficult / thing about learning English?

_____

5 what / expensive / thing / ever / buy?

_____

6 who / important / influence on your life?

_____

7 what / funny / advertisement on TV at the moment?

_____

8 what / useful / *Business know-how* / you / read / so far?

_____

8 Promoting products

1 Read the paragraph then consider the following brands and products. What are their USPs?

Häagen-Dazs ice-cream   the iPod   IKEA   Benetton

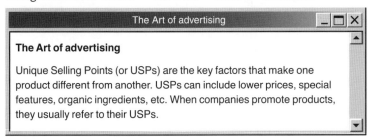

The Art of advertising

Unique Selling Points (or USPs) are the key factors that make one product different from another. USPs can include lower prices, special features, organic ingredients, etc. When companies promote products, they usually refer to their USPs.

2 How do advertisements work? What do they try to do? Note your ideas.

EXAMPLE   *entertain people*

3 Read the article. Did it mention your ideas?

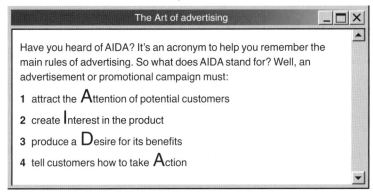

Have you heard of AIDA? It's an acronym to help you remember the main rules of advertising. So what does AIDA stand for? Well, an advertisement or promotional campaign must:

1 attract the Attention of potential customers

2 create Interest in the product

3 produce a Desire for its benefits

4 tell customers how to take Action

4 Match the following with the AIDA checklist.

You want to convince customers of the benefits of having your product.

This may tell people to buy the product by a certain date / tell them when an event will take place / show them how to enter a competition, etc.

A powerful or interesting image, or an attractive special offer, can achieve this.

You can do this by using good headlines and slogans, good design, bright colours, etc.

5 Work in groups. Make a magazine advertisement for a product or brand. Remember to

● advertise the USPs

● refer to AIDA

● include an image

6 Look at the advertisements and decide which advertisement

● is the best (why?)

● attracts your attention the most (why?)

● arouses most interest in the product (how?)

● creates the most desire for its benefits (how?)

● tells customers how to take action most clearly (what action?)

9 Grammar test

1 Write the time expressions below in the correct circle.

three months	*2005*
ten minutes	*ages*
6 o'clock	*two days*
lunchtime	*five years ago*
September	*14 March*
a long time	*this morning*
three hours	*Thursday*
last year	*a week*

for
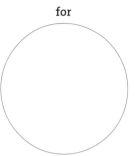

since
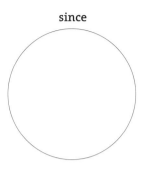

2 Complete the sentences with the correct form of the verb and *for* or *since*.

1 She *has lived* (live) in Berlin *since* 2004.

2 They _____ (not, design) children's clothes _____ three years.

3 Hugo _____ (work) for three fashion houses _____ last year.

4 Gianni and Emilia _____ (run) their own business _____ six months now.

5 He _____ (want) to be involved in fashion _____ he was twelve.

6 It was an amazingly successful show. I _____ (receive) six orders _____ I got into the office.

7 Dee _____ (be) interested in an internship _____ several months.

8 We _____ (attend) all the main fashion shows _____ we set up our own company.

3 Read Karen's notes and write sentences in your notebook about what she hasn't done yet.

Things to do on Tuesday	
~~*brief new intern*~~	*call Andrea*
~~*call accessories manufacturer*~~	*talk to model agency*
book flight to New York	*check new designs*
have lunch with Tara Busch	*reply to Ingrid's email*
send out invitations to fashion show	

4 Answer the questions with *for* or *since*.

1 How long have you been in this language class?

   I've been in this language class for three months.

2 How long have you lived in your present home?

   _____

3 How long have you had your computer?

   _____

4 How long have you studied English?

   _____

5 How long have you been interested in a career in commerce?

   _____

6 How long have you known your English teacher?

   _____

9 Dressing for work

1 People in business tend to wear certain kinds of clothes. Can you describe 'typical' business outfits for a man and a woman?

2 Group the items into the following categories. Some items may fit in more than one column. If any items are specifically for men or women, write M or F.

*jacket   tie   watch   sweatshirt   tiepin   coat   laptop   raincoat   shoes   boots
suit   handbag   ring   sweater   bracelet   shirt   blouse   jeans   backpack
dress   briefcase   necklace   folder   trolley case   T-shirt   cufflinks   umbrella
top   mobile phone   earrings   denim jacket   scarf   smart skirt   socks   belt
shirt   trainers*

Business clothes	Casual clothes	Out and about	Accessories

3 Describe what the people are wearing in the photos.

4 Work in groups and discuss the questions.

- Which of these outfits would be suitable for an interview?
- Are the outfits suitable for all office situations, e.g. meeting a foreign visitor, meetings, routine office work, etc.?
- Which clothes would you feel most comfortable in?

10 Grammar test

1 Complete the sentences using the Present Passive.

1 Our headquarters *are based* (base) in Barcelona.

2 This website _____ (update) every week.

3 Unfortunately, these disks _____ (not, produce) any more.

4 The WWW Consortium _____ (fund) by a number of corporate members.

5 VAT _____ (not, include) in the price.

2 Write sentences using the Past Passive.

1 The contract / signed / yesterday afternoon
The contract was signed yesterday afternoon.

2 The letters / not / deliver / this morning

_____

3 Thousands of orders / generate / the advertising campaign

_____

4 The itinerary / organize / the administrator

_____

5 All my files / corrupt / the virus

_____

6 Last year's conference / not / hold / in Amsterdam

_____

3 Write Passive questions for the following answers.

1 How *is the document sent*?
The document is sent as an email attachment.

2 When _____?
The sales figures were published in January.

3 Where _____?
The printers are manufactured in Japan.

4 What _____?
The company is called Arabesque.

5 How often _____?
We're given appraisals once a year.

4 Complete the text with the verbs in brackets using the Present or Past Passive.

The first charge card

The American businessman Frank McNamara was entertaining clients at a restaurant when he realized that he didn't have his wallet. He 1_____ (allow) by the owners to leave his business card as an IOU. Soon after, he 2_____ (inspire) to invent the charge card. The Diners Club Card 3_____ (launch) in 1950 with only 200 members. They 4_____ (not oblige) to pay cash at 27 New York restaurants but could use their charge card instead. The restaurant bill 5_____ (pay) by the Diners Club, then the cardholder paid the Diners Club at a later date. These days, Diners Club Cards 6_____ (hold) by about eight million people and 7_____ (accept) in over 200 countries.

10 Going online

1 Read the article and discuss the questions.

1 Which is the most important advantage? Which is the least important?
Number them from 1 to 6.

2 Can you think of any other advantages?

Why businesses *go online*

There are many advantages for businesses in going online.

☐ **opportunities for expansion** – businesses can reach lots of new customers

☐ **a global presence** – customers can get information about businesses anywhere in
the world

☐ **looking at the competition** – it is possible for businesses to analyse their
competitors

☐ **equality on the web** – small businesses can look as impressive on the web as big
businesses

☐ **24/7 visibility** – customers can visit a website at any time of the day

☐ **customer contact** – businesses can respond to customers' enquiries very quickly

2 Read the article and answer the questions.

1 How do you think you can make a website 'sticky'? Note ideas from the article
and add your own.

EXAMPLES *update the site regularly   run competitions*

2 Tick the problems you have experienced on websites.

3 Talk about it in groups. Which ones are the most annoying?

'Sticky' websites

'Sticky' sounds like a negative adjective. However, when we talk about 'sticky' websites, it means they are good!
Research suggests that people decide whether they like a website with just two clicks of the mouse. So businesses
try to make their sites as attractive as possible to encourage visitors to stay. There are lots of things they can do,
from creating new content to adding a chat room to creating a newsletter.

Unfortunately, many websites are 'non-stick', and visitors aren't interested in staying – which is bad for business.
There is no point spending money on designing a website if visitors just aren't interested in it.
Here are some of the familiar problems:

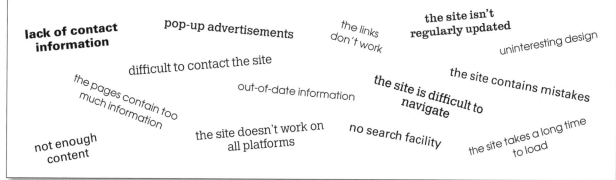

lack of contact information   pop-up advertisements   the links don't work   the site isn't regularly updated   uninteresting design   difficult to contact the site   the pages contain too much information   out-of-date information   the site is difficult to navigate   the site contains mistakes   not enough content   the site doesn't work on all platforms   no search facility   the site takes a long time to load

11 Grammar test

1 Match the beginnings and ends of these sentences.

1 He hasn't been here long,
2 We'll finish by six o'clock,
3 You got a bonus,
4 They're having a meeting,
5 Linda can't do any overtime this week,
6 Roger isn't well organized,
7 They don't regularly work long hours,
8 You're going on a training course tomorrow,
9 He's made lots of suggestions,
10 Guy and Alain arranged the trip,

a can she?
b didn't they?
c is he?
d aren't you?
e hasn't he?
f do they?
g won't we?
h has he?
i didn't you?
j aren't they?

2 Complete the sentences with tag questions.

1 I haven't got all the information here, _have I_?
2 You want to have a job with more responsibility, _____?
3 She thought there was a nice working environment, _____?
4 They won't be able to get here in time, _____?
5 Andrew's going to attend the conference, _____?
6 Their proposal isn't very good, _____?
7 The company offers career breaks of up to two years, _____?
8 We've all studied the report, _____?

3 Complete the sentences. You want your listener to agree with you.

1 You look at the sales figures. You don't think they are very good.
   The sales figures _aren't very good, are they?_
2 Juan hasn't come to the meeting. You think he has forgotten about it.
   Juan _____?
3 You think your listener bought a BlackBerry yesterday.
   You _____?
4 You think Alessia enjoys working in a team.
   Alessia _____?
5 You don't think your company's website is very user-friendly.
   It _____?
6 You think that Lars is thinking of taking early retirement.
   Lars _____?

4 Complete the questions, then ask them to your partner.

1 _____, don't you?
2 _____, haven't you?
3 _____, can you?
4 _____, isn't he?
5 _____, won't they?
6 _____, are we?

11 Flexi-work

1 What are the advantages of working flexible hours for companies and their employees? What are the disadvantages? Note your ideas.

Advantages	Disadvantages

2 Which of your ideas apply to the company (C), employee (E), or both (CE)?

3 Read the magazine article. Underline any of your ideas that the magazine mentions, and add others to your list.

Be flexible

There is a lot of discussion these days about the benefits of flexible working times. Many employers have already introduced it, and in these companies, both employees and their managers agree that there are many advantages. These include greater job satisfaction, people taking fewer days off, and employees managing their workload better. In fact, according to a recent report, employees believe that flexible working time is the key to improving the work-life balance. They say that by making their staff happier in the workplace, managers are able to keep the best talent in their company. So if flexi-work is so good, why aren't more companies introducing it?

Recent polls in all member countries of the European Union suggest that nearly two thirds of companies are not offering flexible working arrangements to their staff. Some employers believe that flexi-work could lead to high costs and losses in productivity. And the doubts aren't only on the employers' side. Some employees don't take up flexi-work because they think it could lead to 'career death'. They think that if they seem to be more interested in their home life than work, it could harm their prospects of promotion.

4 What do you think? Discuss the questions.
- Why are many businesses reluctant to introduce flexi-work?
- Why is there less absenteeism with flexi-work?
- Why could applying for flexible working hours lead to 'career death'?
- Would you want flexible working hours? Why? / Why not?

12 Grammar test

1 Match the beginnings and ends of these sentences.

1 If they increase their prices,
2 If you don't know what to do,
3 Customers will buy more
4 The shop won't survive
5 When they see the results,
6 If our performance doesn't improve,
7 You will discover how people live
8 If we contact Louisa,

a if you examine their rubbish.
b they will be pleasantly surprised.
c they will lose many of their customers.
d we will have to consider redundancies.
e will she be able to help?
f if the shop has a friendly atmosphere.
g unless it improves its layout.
h I'll help you.

2 Re-order the words to write sentences.

1 call you I when I arrive will
   I *will call you when I arrive.*

2 studies pass won't exams she she more her unless
   She _____

3 her reply write to I if you she will sure am
   If _____

4 unless image our harder we won't improve try
   Our _____

5 you if market your use business research improve will
   If _____

6 figures aren't the they do if what good will?
   What _____

7 look promoted I if I will for not another job am
   I _____

8 if help know don't staff what to will you our buy
   If _____

3 Complete the dialogues with the correct form of the verbs. Use short forms.

1 **A** Could I speak to Ms Canfield, please?
   B I'm afraid she isn't in the office, but if you _____ (want) to leave a message, I_____ (see) that she gets it.

2 **A** What _____ (you, do) if you _____ (not, get) a pay rise?
   B I guess I'll have to look for another job.

3 **A** Where shall we meet tomorrow?
   B If you_____ (be able to, get) here by 10.30, I_____ (meet) you at the station.

4 **A** Is this a stressful job?
   B Well, unless you _____ (enjoy) working under pressure, you _____ (not, like) this position.

5 **A** Did our sales increase last month?
   B No, they didn't. And they _____ (only, increase) when we _____ (improve) the quality of our products.

12 Understanding the market

1 Read the article then label the market research techniques Primary (P) or Secondary (S).

Understanding *the market*

Companies need reliable, up-to-date information in order to plan and manage their business. Market trends are changing all the time, so companies need to know what consumers are thinking – and they need to know that fast! Their marketing information comes from primary or secondary sources. In primary market research, companies collect their information directly from customers. With secondary market research, they use information which already exists in printed form, on the Internet, or in computer files.

○ **National newspapers** These carry business sections which can provide useful information and news about market trends.

○ **Personal interviews** These are face-to-face interviews conducted in the street, outside people's homes, or in the workplace. Interviewers usually use questionnaires. It is a popular but expensive method.

○ **Online questionnaires** These are increasingly popular. Questionnaires are either emailed directly to consumers or pop up on websites after customer purchases or enquiries.

○ **Observation** Trained observers watch and analyse consumers' behaviour in various locations.

○ **Printed questionnaires** These are printed in magazines or distributed to homes through the mail. This technique is cheaper than telephoning.

○ **Trade press** These journals provide information for a particular area of business.

○ **Online sources** These include specialist research sites and news sites. Some of these are expensive and not all companies can afford them.

○ **Hall tests** People are brought in from the street to test and discuss a product.

○ **Local newspapers** These contain information which may be useful for local decision-making.

○ **Focus groups** People give their opinions in small groups. This is good for more detailed research.

○ **Telephone interviews** This is a quick and relatively cheap technique. Interviewers use questionnaires. Interviewees often don't want to answer.

○ **Official reports** These may be published by international bodies such as the European Union and national government departments.

○ **Company reports** These include your own company's customer information and reports produced by other businesses.

2 What are the potential benefits and disadvantages of using primary and secondary market research?

EXAMPLE *People may not give true answers in personal interviews.*

3 You work for a market research company. A client wants to set up a new CD and DVD store in your town selling non-mainstream music and films. The client wants to know if it will make money. In groups, decide:

- the information you need to find out (What are the main rival stores? What is the main reason for consumers choosing it? etc.)
- the key people to ask (Which age groups should you focus on? Why? etc.)
- the market research techniques to use (Which ones? Why?)

13 Grammar test

1 Complete the sentences by putting the verbs in brackets into the Past Continuous.

1 They _were studying_ (study) in Budapest in 2004.

2 While you _____ (have) lunch, I thought of a good plan.

3 They _____ (not plan) to change the prototype.

4 We had the idea while we _____ (stand) at the coffee machine.

5 By the end of the last century, McDonald's _____ (operate) in 109 countries.

6 When he invented the 12-digit bar code, Norman Woodland _____ (work) for IBM.

7 Where _____ (you, live) in 1998?

8 She _____ (waiting) for me when I entered the office.

9 I _____ (finish) an important letter when the computer crashed.

10 What _____ (Steve, do) when he came up with the idea?

2 Look at the following sentences. Tick (✔) the correct ones, cross (✗) the wrong ones, and write the correct form of the verbs.

1 | ✗ | Steve Jobs and Stephen Wozniak were meeting at a computer club in California in the 1970s. _met_

2 | ☐ | I worked in the R&D department when I first saw Serge. _____

3 | ☐ | I was logging on to the Internet when the power went off. _____

4 | ☐ | The printer wasn't working when I tried it five minutes ago. _____

5 | ☐ | I had a brilliant idea while I sat in a traffic jam. _____

6 | ☐ | The phone started ringing while I was in a meeting. _____

3 Complete the article by putting the verbs in brackets in the correct tense.

The man who died at his desk

Eric Maplethorpe, an employee in a New York publishing house, _died_ 1 (die) last Tuesday and nobody _____ 2 (notice) for two days! A cleaner _____ 3 (find) Eric dead at his desk on Thursday evening. She _____ 4 (vacuum) the floor when she _____ 5 (ask) him to move his feet. When Eric _____ 6 (not, move) , she _____ 7 (know) something was wrong.

'When I _____ 8 (leave) the office on Thursday, I thought Eric _____ 9 (work) at his desk,' explained a colleague. 'Eric _____ 10 (be) always the first to arrive and the last to leave. He was a quiet man and he _____ 11 (not, talk) much to people.' Eric _____ 12 (correct) a medical text book when he had the heart attack.

4 Answer the questions about you. What were you doing at

1 9.15 a.m. yesterday? _____

2 1 p.m. yesterday? _____

3 8 p.m. yesterday evening? _____

4 6 p.m. last Wednesday? _____

5 11 a.m. last Saturday? _____

6 11 p.m. last Sunday? _____

13 Research and development

1 Read the article and discuss the questions.

1 What are the two main reasons for doing research and development?
2 Can you think of more examples of product improvements?
3 Why would some companies not do any R&D?
4 Why is there more R&D in the computer industry than in the furniture industry?

R&D *the key to the future*

A lot of larger companies have a research and development department. R&D, as it is commonly known, works to improve existing products and develop new ones.

Product improvements are based on market research, and they can include anything from ring-pull cans to memory sticks for computers. New products are either the result of technological advances, such as mobile phones, plasma screens, and Sat Nav (satellite navigation in cars), or innovative new ideas such as Dyson's bagless vacuum cleaner. In some industries where products change very little – for example, the shoe industry – there is not much R&D. However, in high-tech industries where the competition between companies is very intense, there is a constant demand for new products.

But these improvements and innovations come at a price, and countries spend billions of euros of their gross domestic product on R&D. Unfortunately, spending time and money on R&D is no guarantee of success. Around 60% of new products fail in their development – and even when they hit the market, the consumers may not want them. Some products can take up to ten years to develop. By the time they are ready, the world could be a very different place, and the product no longer competitive or relevant. It's a high-risk investment – but the rewards are potentially enormous. Just ask Steve Jobs at Apple.

2 Look at these major new products from the 1930s to the 1990s. Which decade did they come from?

pocket calculator

disposable lighter

suntan lotion

superglue

PlayStation

microwave oven

laptop computer

trainers

DVDs

miniskirt

CDs

3 Work in groups. What possible new products could there be in ten years time? Brainstorm your ideas.

4 Compare your ideas with the rest of the class. Vote for the top three ideas to develop.

14 Grammar test

1 Complete the sentences with the correct form of the verbs.

1 If I _were_ (be) you, I would go home.

2 If we _____ (focus) more on our employees' happiness, we would have a more successful business.

3 Louisa _____ (go) to the conference if you couldn't make it.

4 Alex thinks that if he had a better car he _____ (achieve) bigger sales.

5 If they _____ (invest) more in in-house training, they would soon see the benefits.

6 If I was Teresa, I _____ (not, waste) my time.

7 She _____ (be) much nicer if she were less stressed.

8 If you kept your thoughts on your goals, you _____ (not, get) irritated by small problems.

9 If we _____ (make) customer service a priority, we wouldn't receive so many complaints.

10 If you _____ (have to) choose a new career, what would it be?

2 Underline the correct form of the verbs to complete the sentences.

1 If you _would breath / breathed_ deeply, it _would help / helped_ you to calm down.

2 They _learned / could learn_ a lot about anger management if they _would go / went_ on a course.

3 I _didn't get / wouldn't get_ upset if you _didn't say / wouldn't say_ personal things.

4 She _seemed / wouldn't seem_ so aggressive if she _kept / would keep_ her voice quiet and calm.

5 If you _didn't get / wouldn't get_ the job, _would / will_ you be very disappointed?

6 We _won't be / wouldn't be_ in this crisis if our productivity _was / would be_ higher.

7 If I _were / would be_ her, I _won't talk / wouldn't talk_ to her boss.

8 If we _chose / would choose_ employees with higher EQs, perhaps our overall performance _would be / was_ better.

9 There _wasn't / wouldn't be_ a problem if our boss _wouldn't be / wasn't_ so angry all the time.

10 If I _lived / would live_ in the USA I'm sure I _would speak / spoke_ a lot more fluently.

3 Complete these sentences for you, then compare with a partner.

1 If I had a job with very long hours, I _____ .

2 If I didn't have to work next week, I _____ .

3 If the phone rang at 3 a.m., I _____ .

4 If my best friend criticized my clothes, _____ .

5 If I had to work abroad, I _____ .

6 If I couldn't sleep the night before an important exam, I _____ .

14 Soft skills

1 Do the soft skills quiz.

What are soft skills?

Employers aren't only interested in qualifications and work experience when they interview job candidates. They are also interested in soft skills. You may still be in college or have only recently left – but you already have some soft skills. But what are they? Well, they are things like organizing, planning, using the computer, getting on with people, and coming up with ideas.

What are *your* soft skills? Do our simple quiz and find out!

Give yourself a score from 0 to 3 for each of the skills.

0 poor
1 OK
2 good
3 excellent

Verbal communication skills

Do people listen to you? Are you a good listener?

Examples: speaking one-to-one and in groups, using the telephone, explaining things, listening to people, etc.

My score ☐

Written communication skills

Do you send a lot of emails? Do you enjoy writing?

Examples: printed and online work, writing emails and letters, college essays, stories, and scripts, etc.

My score ☐

Teamwork skills

Do you like working with other people?

Examples: working in a team, team sports, acting in plays, etc.

My score ☐

Practical and mechanical skills

Are you good at fixing things? Do you like using tools?

Examples: using your hands, repairing things, cooking, making things, etc.

My score ☐

Problem-solving skills

Do you do Sudoku? Do you enjoy solving difficult problems?

Examples: coming up with good ideas, planning and organizing, etc

My score ☐

Computer skills

Do you do most of your research on the Internet? Do you use your computer for more than writing?

Examples: word-processing, internet skills, spreadsheets, databases, etc.

My score ☐

Creativity

Do you enjoy painting and drawing? Do you think of better endings to books and films?

Examples: writing stories, doing art, thinking of new ways to do things, etc.

My score ☐

Leadership skills

Do you like taking decisions? Do you enjoy taking responsibility?

Examples: helping people to achieve a task, captaining a sports team, directing a play, etc.

My score ☐

Learning skills

Are you making good progress in your studies? Do you like studying new things?

Examples: learning new things quickly, wanting to learn more skills, learning to play an instrument, etc.

My score ☐

Time management skills

Do you keep up with all your work?

Examples: keeping to a schedule, meeting deadlines, giving in your homework on time, etc.

My score ☐

Your soft skills rating

24-30 Amazing! Why aren't you running your own successful business already?

16-23 Very good! You will impress any interviewer with these skills. Keep on adding to your skills base.

6-15 Not bad. You have enough soft skills to get an employer interested, but try to develop more.

0-5 Oh dear! Perhaps you should concentrate on getting qualifications!

2 Discuss your answers with a partner. How can you improve some of your soft skills?

15 Grammar test

1 Write the words in the correct order.

1 may at I tomorrow home work

  I may work at home tomorrow.

2 offer the will him she job

  _____

3 move Germany to they not might

  _____

4 promoted may be not Nikola

  _____

5 definitely the year will company next restructure

  _____

6 that might thinks redundant made he be he

  _____

2 Complete these sentences with the correct modal verb in brackets.

1 You must apply for this job. You *may not* (may / may not) see a better one.

2 I'll try to change the flight but it _____ (won't / might not) be possible.

3 If you take risks, you _____ (may / will) probably make some mistakes.

4 We _____ (may / may not) be able to go to the sales conference. We're very busy at the moment.

5 Look at my bank statement! I _____ (won't / may not) buy any more things online!

6 I don't know what to do. I _____ (won't / might not) go to the interview.

7 OK, that's arranged. I _____ (will / might) see you at 9.30 tomorrow.

8 If we offer David the job, do you think he _____ (may / will) accept it?

3 Complete the dialogues with *will, won't, might,* or *might not*.

1 **A** *Will* you let me know if they offer you a pay rise?

  B Of course I _____!

2 **A** Are they still in the meeting?

  B Yes, they aren't going to finish today. We _____ have to wait until tomorrow before they reach an agreement.

3 **A** Are you going to leave the office on time today?

  B Well, if I finish writing all these letters, I _____!

4 **A** What are you doing at the weekend?

  B I'm not sure. I _____ do anything, actually. I feel too tired.

5 **A** Have you called Ana?

  B Yes, there was no answer. She _____ still be on her way to work.

6 **A** I _____ be able to go out tonight. It depends if I finish my work.

  B Well, I hope you can make it!

7 **A** _____ you apply for the job?

  B Yes, I think I probably _____.

8 **A** Hi, Femke! I'm calling from the station.

  B Hi, Martin! Listen, I _____ be able to pick you up. Take a taxi and remember to ask for a receipt.

15 Interview techniques

1 Read the article and match the questions with the advice.

The Interview Doctor
Dr Helen Anderson

Interviews can be difficult, stressful, and unpleasant. However, if you are prepared, you can turn even the most difficult questions to your advantage. So here is my advice for answering five of the trickiest interview questions.

1   Tell me about yourself.

2   Where do you see yourself in five years' time?

3   How do you cope with working under pressure?

4   What are your weaknesses?

5   Why should I employ you?

DR HELEN SAYS ...

☐ A   This is a difficult question. In the interview you are already under pressure and the interviewer can see how you are coping! However, it's always a good idea to say that you quite like pressure and stress, that it makes work more exciting and interesting, etc. Also think of things that you do to help you relax.

☐ B   This is your opportunity to talk about your strengths and positive qualities. Say why you are good for the job. Mention any good work you have done in the past or any positive feedback you have received. Talk about your skills.

☐ C   Don't give too many examples of these! However, either mention a weakness that the interviewer could think is a strength (*I can sometimes get too involved in my work and forget to go home*) or think of a strength that you have that cancels it (*I sometimes don't concentrate in meetings ... but it's because I'm thinking of new ideas*).

☐ D   This is a terrible question. The interviewer wants to know about you – but he / she doesn't want to know what you had for breakfast or what you're doing that evening. Try to keep your answer to talking about your career, relevant experience, and qualifications.

☐ E   This is your opportunity to talk about your ambitions that relate to this particular job interview. The interviewer wants to know how the company will benefit from employing you. Don't suggest that you want to take your manager's job. That could be a big mistake!

2 How would you answer these questions? Discuss your ideas with a partner.

3 Look at the job advertisement. What qualities do you need for the job?

> ## ASSISTANT AT TRADE FAIR
>
> The successful applicants must:
> - deal with the public
> - speak English
> - work in a team
> - be prepared to work long hours

4 Work in groups. Imagine that you are attending a job interview for the trade fair assistant job. Take it in turns to be the interviewer and interviewee.

- Ask the questions to different students.
- Decide who gave the best answers and why.

Grammar tests key

Unit 1

1 2 doesn't allow
3 arrives
4 gets
5 don't sell
6 prefer
7 doesn't have
8 studies
9 sends
10 don't have

2 2 does she start
3 does he work
4 Do they enjoy working
5 do they take
6 are your main responsibilities
7 does Andrew use
8 do you take
9 Does Ella mind
10 do you finish

3 2 He doesn't like using technology.
3 He doesn't mind working in a team.
4 He hates doing research.
5 He's good at dealing with people.

Unit 2

1 2 does your department do?
3 aren't achieving
4 want
5 organize
6 is Sebastian doing, 's doing
7 never misses
8 is
9 are you writing
10 flies

2 2 'm travelling
3 don't usually have
4 is
5 have
6 'm learning
7 seem
8 often go out
9 hope
10 are having

3 2 work
3 are you doing
4 'm developing
5 's
6 's driving
7 's he seeing
8 're talking
9 are Ben and Katie doing
10 's talking
11 isn't / 's not
12 's visiting

Unit 3

1 2 took
3 came
4 travelled
5 read
6 stood
7 applied
8 went
9 planned
10 worked
11 bought
12 found

2 2 started
3 Did Louise pack
4 missed
5 met
6 did they choose

3 2 We waited at the station for more than two hours but the train didn't arrive.
3 Did Mr Janssen sign the contract yesterday?
4 She tried to call on her mobile but she wasn't able to get a signal.
5 I forgot to buy the tickets.
6 Why didn't Melissa apply for that job?

4 2 went
3 finished
4 was
5 didn't work
6 didn't clean
7 wasn't able to
8 didn't serve
9 was
10 watched
11 did you do
12 slept

Unit 4

1 1 B I got here at about quarter past nine.

2 A Have you ever considered a career in sport?

B Yes, I have. In fact, I worked in a gym two years ago.

3 A What did you do at the training course yesterday?

B We learnt how to run effective meetings.

4 A Have they ever gone / been to the USA before?

B Yes, they have. They went a couple of years ago.

2 2 started   10 followed

3 've been   11 showed

4 have you covered   12 enjoyed

5 've worked   13 Have you seen

6 've answered   14 watched

7 've also helped   15 do you want

8 Have you worked   16 haven't worked

9 was

3 2 ✓   4 ✓   6 ✗ I trained

3 ✗ I've put   5 ✗ hasn't run

Unit 5

1 2 'm meeting   6 aren't planning

3 are/'re having   7 are/'re visiting

4 are/'re going   8 Is Gary joining

5 are/'re attending   9 are we seeing

2 2 Alan is going to improve his sales technique.

3 Marie isn't going to send more than ten text messages a day.

4 Alan is going to set clearer targets.

5 They re going to leave work before 7.

6 They are going to apply for a new job.

3 2 Are you doing   6 'm meeting

3 are falling   7 'm not going to write

4 isn't going to like   8 aren't increasing

5 Is she going to take

Unit 6

1 2 must arrive   5 must avoid   7 mustn't eat

3 mustn't stare 6 must be   8 must stand

4 must take off

2 2 don't have to   6 mustn't

3 mustn't   7 doesn't have to

4 mustn't   8 mustn't

5 don't have to

3 2 You mustn't say

3 I have to deal with

4 I must / have to

5 Did you have to leave

6 He must remember

7 Applicants don't have to have

8 We had to go

9 Do you have to, I must / have to be

10 Visitors mustn't leave

Unit 7

1 2 should have, should use

3 shouldn't forget

4 should keep on, shouldn't change

5 should get

2 2 What do you think we should take?

3 Where should I put the files?

4 Do you think I should ask for a pay rise?

5 How long do you think she should stay at the conference?

6 Who should they send the documents to?

Unit 8

1 2 more competitive, most competitive

3 bigger, biggest

4 more effective, most effective

5 farther / further, farthest / furthest

6 costlier, costliest

7 worse, worst

8 more interesting, most interesting

9 simpler, simplest

10 hotter, hottest

2 2 the most effective
3 the most expensive
4 cheaper
5 smaller
6 more exciting
7 the fastest
8 the cheapest
9 the best
10 easier

3 Students write their own answers to the following questions.

2 What's the best advertisement you have ever seen?

3 Who's the most famous business person in your country?

4 What's the most difficult thing about learning English?

5 What's the most expensive thing you've ever bought?

6 Who's the most important influence on your life?

7 What's the funniest advertisement on TV at the moment?

8 What's the most useful *Business know-how* you have read so far?

Unit 9

1 **for** three months ten minutes ages a week two days a long time three hours

since 2005 last year Thursday 6 o'clock lunchtime five years ago September 14 March this morning

2 2 haven't designed, for
3 has worked, since
4 have run, for
5 has wanted, since
6 have received, since
7 has been, for
8 have attended, since

3 She hasn't booked a flight to New York yet.

She hasn't had lunch with Tara Busch yet.

She hasn't called Andrea yet.

She hasn't talked to the model agency yet.

She hasn't checked the new designs yet.

She hasn't replied to Ingrid's email yet.

She hasn't sent out invitations to the fashion show yet.

Unit 10

1 2 is updated
3 aren't produced
4 is funded
5 isn't included

2 2 The letters weren't delivered this morning.

3 Thousands of orders were generated by the advertising campaign.

4 The itinerary was organized by the administrator.

5 All my files were corrupted by the virus.

6 Last year's conference wasn't held in Amsterdam.

3 2 When were the sales figures published?
3 Where are the printers manufactured?
4 What is the company called?
5 How often are we given appraisals?

4 1 was allowed
2 was inspired
3 was launched
4 weren't obliged
5 was paid
6 are held
7 are accepted
8 was introduced

Unit 11

1 2 g 3 i 4 j 5 a 6 c 7 f 8 d 9 e 10 b

2 2 don't you
3 didn't she
4 will they
5 isn't he
6 is it
7 doesn't it
8 haven't we

3 2 Juan's forgotten to come to the meeting, hasn't he?

3 You bought a BlackBerry yesterday, didn't you?

4 Alessia enjoys working in a team, doesn't she?

5 It isn't very user-friendly, is it?

6 Lars is thinking of taking early retirement, isn't he?

Unit 12

1 2 h 3 f 4 g 5 b 6 d 7 a 8 e

2 2 She won't pass her exams unless she studies more.

3 If I write to her, I am sure she will reply.

4 Our image won't improve unless we try harder.

5 If you use market research, your business will improve.

6 What will they do if the figures aren't good?

7 I will not look for another job if I am promoted.

8 If you don't know what to buy, our staff will help.

3 1 want, 'll see

2 will you do, don't get

3 're able to get, 'll meet

4 enjoy, won't like

5 'll only increase, improve

Unit 13

1 2 were having

3 weren't planning

4 were standing

5 were operating

6 was working

7 were you living

8 was waiting

9 was finishing

10 was Steve doing

2 2 ✗ was working

3 ✓

4 ✓

5 ✗ was sitting

6 ✓

3 2 noticed   8 left

3 found   9 was working

4 was vacuuming   10 was

5 asked   11 didn't talk

6 didn't move   12 was correcting

7 knew

Unit 14

1 2 focused

3 could / would go

4 would achieve

5 invested

6 wouldn't waste

7 would be

8 wouldn't get

9 made

10 had to

2 2 could learn, went

3 wouldn't get, didn't say

4 wouldn't seem, kept

5 didn't get, would

6 wouldn't be, was

7 were, wouldn't talk

8 chose, would be

9 wouldn't, wasn't

10 lived, would speak

Unit 15

1 2 She will offer him the job.

3 They might not move to Germany.

4 Nikola may not be promoted.

5 The company will definitely restructure next year.

6 He thinks that he might be made redundant.

2 2 might not   6 might not

3 will   7 will

4 may not   8 will

5 won't

3 1 will   5 might

2 will   6 might not

3 will   7 Will, will

4 might not   8 won't